CAPITALISM ON EDGE

NEW DIRECTIONS IN CRITICAL THEORY

NEW DIRECTIONS IN CRITICAL THEORY

AMY ALLEN, GENERAL EDITOR

New Directions in Critical Theory presents outstanding classic and contemporary texts in the tradition of critical social theory, broadly construed. The series aims to renew and advance the program of critical social theory, with a particular focus on theorizing contemporary struggles around gender, race, sexuality, class, and globalization and their complex interconnections.

For a complete list of titles, see page 255.

CAPITALISM ON EDGE

HOW FIGHTING PRECARITY CAN ACHIEVE RADICAL CHANGE WITHOUT CRISIS OR UTOPIA

ALBENA AZMANOVA

Columbia University Press   *New York*

Columbia University Press
Publishers Since 1893
New York   Chichester, West Sussex
cup.columbia.edu
Copyright © 2020 Columbia University Press
All rights reserved

Library of Congress Cataloging-in-Publication Data

Names: Azmanova, Albena, author.
Title: Capitalism on edge : how fighting precarity can achieve radical
change without crisis or utopia / Albena Azmanova.
Description: New York : Columbia University Press, [2020] | Series: New
directions in critical theory | Includes bibliographical references and index.
Identifiers: LCCN 2019020917 (print) | LCCN 2019981142 (ebook) |
ISBN 9780231195362 (cloth) | ISBN 9780231195379 (paperback) |
ISBN 9780231530606 (ebook)
Subjects: LCSH: Capitalism. | Equality.
Classification: LCC HB501 .A96 2020 (print) | LCC HB501 (ebook) |
DDC 330.12/2—dc23
LC record available at https://lccn.loc.gov/2019020917
LC ebook record available at https://lccn.loc.gov/2019981142

Cover design: Milenda Nan Ok Lee
Cover image: Interesni Kazki, *The Sysyphus* (2010). Mural painting,
Ekaterinburg, Russia.

Hope is definitely not the same thing as optimism. It is not the conviction that something will turn out well, but the certainty that something makes sense, regardless of how it turns out.

—Václav Havel, *The Politics of Hope* (1986)

The concept of crisis would be the signature of a last symptom, the convulsive effort to save "a world" that we no longer inhabit.

—Jacques Derrida, "Economies of the Crisis" (1983)

To be radical is to grasp things by the root.

—Karl Marx, *A Contribution to the Critique of Hegel's Philosophy of Right* (1844)

CONTENTS

PREFACE

A joke was circulating in the Soviet bloc in the 1980s, just as the socialist dictatorships were about to collapse: "Capitalism stands on the brink of the abyss. It will soon be overtaken by communism." Much to everyone's surprise, this indeed came to pass. The "brave new world" of autocratic socialism has long since tumbled off the cliff. Today, capitalism is still facing the abyss as an accumulation of ecological, social, and economic problems have put it on edge, if not quite brought it to the edge of its existence.

These dissident jokes did not mean to amuse, but rather they gave us a delightful sense of teasing the political common sense of the day. This book is about the possibilities for radical change, of unsettling and unseating capitalism, despite its thriving through seemingly endless crises. It is meant to share with the reader the pleasure of discerning the common sense behind the apparently unthinkable—easing our way out of capitalism without necessarily embracing socialism.

Capitalism and socialism have been the two competing systems that aspired to deliver well-being for all. In pursuing that goal, they severely damaged an indispensable condition of well-being, the natural environment. Nowadays, even the most mature democratic societies are failing to deliver on their commitment to fighting climate change. This brings up some uncomfortable questions: Are the political and economic systems that have facilitated environmental devastation capable of fixing it? If the answer is no, do we have an alternative?

Our times are bereft of great crises, revolutionary upheavals, and utopias. Yet never before have the conditions been so ripe for overcoming capitalism—without the help of crisis, revolution, or utopia. Radical progressive change without a revolutionary break is possible, and the time is right for it, as this book sets out to demonstrate.

I was personally involved in the short life of autocratic socialism (or the "communist regime," as it is often called), and helped make it shorter as I became involved with the dissident movements and student strikes that challenged it in my native Bulgaria. But we did not rebel against communism; neither did we hunger after capitalism. Our discontent was imbued with a sense that the everyday reality we inhabited was somehow pathological, as it deviated much too far from the ideals of humanism, fraternity, and decency the system purported to embody. There was, I remember, a lot of talk at that time about things being "not normal"—the ruling class was corrupt and ignorant, the privileges of elites appalling, the restrictions on freedom of speech absurd, and the austerity of living distressing, because it was austerity for most, enabling the affluence of some. Our requests did not seem radical; they were in line with the blueprint of communism as a fair and free society. That is why I was taken aback when, on a spring day in 1988, my Head of School told me that I was to be expelled from the university because I had joined an organization that "did not have the blessing of the Party." The day before, I had unwittingly become an enemy of the regime by simply signing a petition that called for stopping life-threatening pollution in a city on the Danube River—hardly a threat to the establishment. The regime itself had turned our commonsense demands for safeguarding human life and the environment into an antiestablishment action—much as is happening now with the youth climate marches and the Green New Deal.

When the dictatorships in Eastern Europe rapidly collapsed in 1989, there was no strategy, no grand plan for the aftermath, no organized revolutionary force, and not even much of a crisis of the regime except some troubles in the economy, akin to the post-2008 recession in Western democracies. The recently declassified secret service files revealed that the regime did not consider rebels like me a serious threat. ("They are good communists" was the assessment.) Yet the multiplicity of our seemingly innocent and uncoordinated pressures had put socialism on edge. Without knowing it, we were living on the edge of socialism. Eventually, our actions did trigger a radical and irreversible change that issued a whole new political and economic order.

Years later, first as a student of politics in New York and then as a professor in Paris and Brussels, I spent much of my time marveling at the failed promises and unfulfilled failures of capitalist democracies: from women's almost-successful struggles for equality with men and the perpetually reemerging "religious question" in secular democracies to the notorious crisis of capitalism that never quite materialized. The proliferation of almost-achievements (prosperity, but not for all) and incomplete failures (environmental near-catastrophe), the confluence of the unprecedented technological capacity for life improvement with the anxiety engulfing whole societies—all these contradictory trends have brought democratic capitalism to a moment of reckoning. The writing of this book was prompted by a sense of political déjà vu: a revolution in the West is hardly in the offing, yet the potential for radical change is acutely present.

A decade after the financial meltdown of 2007–2008, even as the United States and Europe have begun to return to their pre-crisis growth, these societies are beset by a broad, nebulous discontent, shared even by some of the champions of capitalism. Something is amiss, say business magnate–turned-president Donald Trump and Christine Lagarde, managing director of the International Monetary Fund. Indeed, much is not right, agree the millions of people who are losing livelihoods as a result of the way the likes of Trump and Lagarde are shaping our world.

On the streets and in electoral booths, from demonstrations against austerity policies to the rise of electoral support for anti-establishment parties, the upsurge of social protest in the early twenty-first century has made it clear that we can no longer accept being told that "there is no alternative." We, the denizens of liberal democracies, have finally lost some of our political credulity.

This book makes a simple claim: The current state of capitalist democracy contains a tangible potential for overcoming capitalism by *subverting* it. This is a different path of change compared with *stabilizing* it (as per calls coming from the political Right), *overthrowing* it (as per appeals by the radical Left), or *reforming* it to make it more humane (the ambition of the center-left). *Subverting* capitalism is a matter of performing changes from within by implementing practices that strike at the driving force of capitalism—the competitive production of profit—the very dynamic that is destroying human existence, communities, and our natural environment. Such a process of subversion, I contend, does not depend on a deliberate and politically articulated endorsement of socialism or any other vision of good society as an alternative to capitalism. Just like the transition from feudalism to capitalism did not proceed under the aegis of a grand design called "capitalism," the current possibility for an exit from capitalism does not demand a guiding theoretical elaboration of postcapitalism.

I am aware that my sense of history is affected and, I hope, made more alert by my personal experience with unseating autocratic socialism. These intuitions about the current historical juncture of capitalist democracies have matured into an analysis through some fifteen years of research. My thinking has been much affected by the work of (and often debates with and written comments by) Claus Offe, Robert Reich, Nancy Fraser, Wolfgang Streeck, Kalypso Nikolaidis, Étienne Balibar, Jodi Dean, Peter Fleming, Andreas Kalyvas, Wendy Brown, Costas Douzinas, Seyla Benhabib, Steven Lukes, Maeve Cooke, Michael Leigh, Amy Allen, Rainer Forst, Peter Hall, David Rasmussen, Alessandro Ferrara, Andrew Feenberg, Victor Elgersma, Mirella Elgersma, and my comrades in the Radical Critical Theory Circle, as well as my students at the University of Kent, to mention just a few of the people who have nourished and teased my thinking. I am particularly indebted to Anastas Gueordjev and Jacqueline Cessou for their apt editorial intervention and to Victor Elgersma for his insightful research assistance throughout my writing. One of the most felicitous outcomes of these preparatory investigations was the emergence of the "Brussels group" of the Frankfurt School, as Azar Dakwar, Raphael Wolf, Daniel Lopez Perez, and I worked together on our separate projects—spanning work, protest, religion, security, and civil war—through a critique of contemporary capitalism. Finally, the team at Columbia University Press—their smart counsel and patient enthusiasm for this project brought joy where frustration normally reigns.

One of my teachers, the great historian Eric Hobsbawm, used to say to us that history books should not be written for historians, just as philosophy books should not be written just for other philosophers. By pitching my style of reflection in the middle road between the initiated and the novice, I aspire to follow his advice. Of course, some knowledge of history and philosophy may make the reading more enjoyable, but it is my hope that the lack of it will not stand in the way of understanding.

My analyses draw on history, political theory, and political economy. Initially, I was doubtful about this disciplinary admixture. I came, however, to endorse it, not only because it befits the subject matter of this book, but also because I realized that my own idiosyncratic schooling has enabled it, and I should indeed profit from it. I am fortunate to have studied with some of the best minds in these fields: Claus Offe, Nancy Fraser, Andrew Arato, Seyla Benhabib, Ira Katznelson, Aristide Zolberg, Charles Tilly, Eric Hobsbawm, Charles Larmore, Ronald Dworkin, and Joseph Raz. All the wisdom of these scholars, however, would likely have been lost on me without the subversively enlightening work of three of my teachers from the time of the "old regime" in Bulgaria: Georgi Dimitrov, Evgenii Dainov, and Stefan Popov. I eagerly acknowledge my debt to all of them. Were I not afraid of sounding presumptuous, I would dedicate this book to them.

INTRODUCTION

"How Come?" Asked the Befuddled Left

The best way to make your dreams come true is to wake up.
—Paul Valéry, *Tel Quel* (1941)

Remember the "roaring nineties"—the world's most prosperous decade?[1] Even as the twentieth century thus gloriously inaugurated the twenty-first, and long before the inglorious financial-economic-social crisis of 2007–2008 beset Europe and the United States, a wave of puzzling developments began to emerge. One such enigma was presented to me in 2002 by a grouping of Left parties at the European Parliament, who asked the following question: "How come, despite good economic performance and low unemployment, ruling Left parties have been losing elections across Europe?" I agreed to look into the matter, and eventually did find an answer, but not one that my interlocutors liked: under the impact of globally integrated markets and automation, capitalism was undergoing a rapid transformation, generating new social concerns that the European political establishment of center-left and center-right parties, and also the radical Left, were ignoring, thus allowing new and reformed antiestablishment parties to give vent to the growing public discontent.[2] I advised the Left to promptly wake up to this reality if it was to remain politically relevant.

That, however, seemed to me a precipitous, if plausible, answer to an important question that merited further examination. I therefore continued my research in subsequent years, canvassing the whole spectrum of the change I had detected, from the political economy of Western democracies to the ideological landscape and predominant styles of social protest and intellectual critique. This book brings together the various strands of my investigation to put forth a story about the transformation of democratic capitalism in the early twenty-first century. This is a tale about the mutation of what has come to be known as "neoliberal capitalism" into the new, more malignant form of capitalist society we inhabit today. I call this *precarity capitalism* in order to highlight one of its distinctive features—the universalization of insecurity, which is now afflicting the majority of the population, almost irrespective of employment type and income level.

While much has been said in recent years about the crisis of capitalism and its impending collapse, I offer an alternative story here: that capitalism as an engine of prosperity is doing well. Yet we do not need a grand crisis, a revolution, or a utopia to transcend it. This book traces both the inexistent crisis of capitalism amid much emphatic talk of crisis, and the existing possibilities of its radical overcoming.

In the pages that follow, I will claim that, despite fears and anticipations of the crisis of capitalism, no such crisis has taken place. What are commonly seen as its manifestations—from the rise of populism to the upsurge of precarious employment and slacking of growth—are, rather, the "growing pains" in a process of transforming capitalism from the neoliberal model to the precarity form. In fact, the very discourse about the crisis of capitalism is significant. As Jacques Derrida cautioned, it is precisely when "the idea that the present world is in crisis is experiencing its greatest inflation" that we must be suspicious and ask, "Who is talking about crisis? Who is talking the most about it right now? To whom? In what form? In view of what effects and what interests?" (1983, 71).

Curiously, as I will discuss in chapter 1, both the neoliberal Right and the radical Left have indulged in the discourse of crisis of capitalism, even as they endorse two opposing connotations—fears over capitalism's impending collapse or hopes for its imminent demise. On the political Right, this is about a temporary, yet dangerous disorder of a mechanism that is allegedly essential for societies' well-being, something worth saving by means of giving even more power to economic and political elites. This conception has spurred a plethora of policies aimed at healing capitalism (e.g., cutting public spending to appease financial markets). This conservative use of the discourse of crisis has its counterpart on the radical Left, which hopes for capitalism's collapse through self-inflicted cardiac arrest, one triggered by rampant inequality, greedy bankers, and reckless rulers. In this version, capitalism is meant to "dig its own grave" as the actions of its political and economic leadership spark massive insurrections. What these twin versions of the crisis of capitalism obscure in their hasty diagnoses is the transformation of the sociopolitical order and the emergence of forms of suffering and injustice for which the old lexicon of progressive politics—which saw injustice mainly as a matter of inequalities and exclusion—has no available concepts. Even worse, they ignore the possibility for radical transformation without the crutch of a crisis, revolution, or utopia.

I propose that we shed our fascination with the crisis of capitalism and instead focus our attention on the singularity of our time in order to discern tendencies that contain opportunities for *overcoming* capitalism, rather than stabilizing or overthrowing it. However, this book offers neither predictions about nor prescriptions for life after capitalism. It instead traces an observable pattern, first of the transformation of neoliberal capitalism into a new form and then of tendencies and tangible trajectories of a radical change—of overcoming capitalism by subverting it.

This book is driven as much by an awareness of available prospects for radical change as by an anxiety that progressive forces are now taking the wrong path, reviving the familiar formula of the "class struggle" in their calls for saving democracy by taxing the rich. Indeed, the political and economic oligarchies that have emerged over the past thirty years, as well as the intensified assault on liberal values by protofascist movements, have done terrible damage to our societies. Democracy needs to be fortified as a matter of emergency. But I believe we can do more. In order to shed light on a path that leads beyond the democratization of capitalism, I recast the critique of capitalism to focus more firmly on the dynamics of the competitive production of profit. Central to my analysis is a notion of "radical practice" that counters these dynamics, which are constitutive of capitalism. I spell out this model in chapter 2. Although this book is intended for a readership beyond the academic community, I am an academic and cannot help but include one chapter in which I expose in detail the logic and logistics of my analysis. However, this chapter is freestanding. Readers who are averse to theory may proceed directly to the body of the analysis in the subsequent chapters. The appendix provides a quick reference for terms such as "emancipation paradox" that are discussed more fully in chapter 2.

I owe the reader an early disclosure of my take on capitalism. On the question of socialism and capitalism, I've always shared the views of Czech writer, statesman, and former dissident Václav Havel that "these thoroughly ideological and often semantically confused categories have long since been beside the point." ([1984] 1991, 263). However, in order to discuss the range and nature of the impulses Western societies now contain for radical change, I treat these societies as institutional orders that combine democracy as a political system with capitalism as a social system. I therefore speak of *democratic capitalism* as a particular institutionalized social order comprising these two mutually entwined systems, each with its particular operative logic, enabling structures, and distributive outcomes. By "system," I mean structured social relations—relations that are generated through actors' mundane interactions in the course of everyday social practices (such as working or paying the bills) and stabilized by the rules that regulate these practices. I do not hold that there is an "objective system" completely independent of actors' volition. Such a view would make us all captive to a fate we could not escape; even worse, it would exculpate the perpetrators of injustice as being themselves innocent victims of an anonymous system. For current purposes, however, it is useful to think of the present historical conundrum in terms of the effects of a system, for the simple reason that capitalist democracies exhibit the symptoms of systems, with their distinct core logics of the competitive generation of profit and the competitive acquisition of political office. These systems and the social order they constitute are brought to life through rules and institutions, and they can be critiqued, criticized, opposed, and undone.

As I will clarify in chapter 2, this Marxian (but not Marxist)[3] understanding of capitalism as a historically specific and evolving system of social relations sets it apart from its facile reduction to a "market economy," the production and consumption of goods exchanged through the market. The holistic conceptualization I endorse—of democratic capitalism as an institutionalized social order and of capitalism as a social system within that order—places the focus on the practices through which society reproduces itself. This shifts attention away from an exclusive focus on social relations of *class*, a perspective that is predominant among Marxist scholars and sets the tone of the current Left criticism of neoliberalism. Such thinkers perceive the injustice of capitalism exclusively as a matter of class or group domination. Their attention is on the distribution of life-chances in society. I propose that we be particularly vigilant about the formation of life-chances. What constitutes a successful life under capitalism? How does this make certain scenarios of action politically viable? We can find the answers by examining the core logics and institutional logistics of the competitive production of profit and the diverse forms of harm it inflicts on human beings, societies, and nature. This will allow us to treat experiences of injustice not just as grievances of victims claiming redress (for, say, being underpaid or disrespected), but as pointing, in the diversity of such experiences, to a distress that can be traced to the overarching logic of the social system. This attention to systemic dynamics rather than material inequalities and structures of ownership will lead me to observe the unprecedented cumulation of injustices among the "99 percent," as well as to single out precarity as the common denominator among the diverse grievances. It is here that tangible possibilities reside for mobilizing a resistance (counter-hegemony) against the driving force of capitalism and eventually subverting it by using the institutions of liberal democracy.

Let me now trace the progression of my investigation through the seven chapters of this book. My point of departure, in chapter 1, is the discourse of "crisis of capitalism" that emerged in the aftermath of the 2007–2008 economic meltdown. I trace the deflation of the narrative of a grand, terminal crisis of capitalism and the rise of one about the unfairness of inequalities, which has spurred calls for redistribution across the left–right political divide. This shift suggests something significant about the nature of the "legitimacy deal" between citizens and public authority—that is, what citizens consider to be valuable services the state can and must perform for society. What is being *obscured* in the preselection of grievances deemed worthy of political notice is an equally significant part of the legitimacy deal. Why have pressures increased on the state to deliver economic justice by reducing inequality rather than by alleviating poverty or providing stable employment? This invites us to take a closer look at the selective *process of politicization*—that is, the way society's afflictions, from unemployment to lack of physical safety and growing economic uncertainty, are or are not being presented as issues demanding political attention and policy action. The theme of politicization will be central to my investigation: namely, which social problems are considered deserving of public attention, and how social anxieties become political problems worthy of policy action.

The unfairness of inequality has become the dominant frame of social protest since the Occupy movement proudly stated, "We are the 99 percent." I take this indignation, which I address in the first chapter, to be a symptom not of the crisis of capitalism but rather of its unfailing good health. This is the case because remonstrations against inequality present the matter of capitalism's numerous and grave failures as issues that can be easily tackled with a dose of redistributive policies and strengthened oversight. Thus, what appears to be a radical challenge to neoliberal capitalism is instead a reinforcement of it, as we inevitably validate the model of life into which we seek equal inclusion—what I describe as "the paradox of emancipation." Public protests thus unwittingly relegitimize the social system they purport to challenge as they seek to diminish the inequalities neoliberalism has engendered without addressing the root causes of the economic and social crisis. (Note that the growth of inequality was an outcome of this crisis, not a cause of it.) Thus, capitalism has continued to prosper despite growing public dissatisfaction. Its economic engine is having considerable difficulties with delivering growth and prosperity *for all*, yet the legitimacy deal in Western societies has been altered so as to endow it with renewed authority. There is no crisis of capitalism. We inhabit, instead, a *crisis of the crisis of capitalism*, as I shall suggest.

The deflation of social protest (that is, the shift from the discourse of crisis of capitalism to calls for redistribution) and the conservative, defensive nature of the protests are symptomatic of a thorough transmutation of the socioeconomic model of Western capitalist democracies. While we have been debating the crisis of capitalism, neoliberal capitalism has not only survived the economic recession of the second decade of our century, but has also completed a transformation that had begun before the financial crisis set in. I will trace this mutation of neoliberalism into the even more noxious form I have named "precarity capitalism" for reasons that will become clear as the story unfolds.

In chapter 3, I trace the formation of political ideologies and the reshaping of the electoral mobilization map as this new form of capitalism finds its shape. This includes the obliteration, since the beginning of the current century, of the classical left–right divide by an opportunity–risk divide that cuts across old loyalties and forges unlikely new alliances. These shifts have been fostered by perceptions of the impact of the new economy of open borders and technological innovation as either opportunities or risks, which have then been expressed as public concerns (e.g., immigration, loss of livelihood, or our carbon footprint). The old center-left and center-right political formations are now converging into an "opportunity" pole formed by perceptions of the benefits of market openness and technocratic policymaking, while the former extremes of the political spectrum are converging around a "risk" pole that unites people who reject what Vermont senator Bernie Sanders called "establishment politics and establishment economics." I draw on evidence from political mobilization and electoral politics in the United States and Europe in order to discern the emergence of a new set of public demands to which the political supply by parties is currently responding. This understanding offers an alternative to narratives about the rise (and implied fall) of populism. The idea of a populist insurgency connotes an interlude, a temporary deviation from "normal politics." This is not my interpretation of the phenomenon, and I have proposed that we abstain from using the term "populism" altogether. Positioning the allegedly populist upheavals within this new but stable reconfiguration of the ideological landscape of capitalist democracies will allow us to discern a road ahead.

Yet the fact that new fault lines are emerging in electoral combat and public debates does not necessarily mean that an opposition to neoliberal capitalism is brewing "from below." Nor does it imply that the social forces currently supporting the policy status quo have an enduring interest in continuing that support. In order to examine the potential for a radical transformation, in chapter 5 I survey the political economy and state–society relations of the new form of capitalism. To highlight its peculiarities, in the previous chapter I offer a brief review of its preceding forms, namely nineteenth-century liberal capitalism, early twentieth-century welfare capitalism, and the neoliberal formula of the late twentieth century. Let me make clear that I harbor no facile negative judgment when speaking of capitalism and any of its modalities. Although I draw upon many of the intellectual critiques that have turned "neoliberalism" into a pejorative term, my analysis views all forms of capitalism as intertwined dynamics of emancipation (that is, alleviation of oppression) and domination, as per Marx's original analysis. The point is to detect progressive tendencies while bringing to view the oppressive and exploitative processes at work.

In chapter 6, I address the possibility, even the likelihood, of a different sort of radical change—in the articulation of an overarching interest that the "99 percent" have developed in making significant changes to the socioeconomic system they inhabit. Policy responses to their multiple grievances would result in a gradual exiting from capitalism because they would inhibit the very constitutive logic of capitalism—namely, the competitive pursuit and production of profit. Chapter 7 articulates the politics and policies of this transformation as building what I call "a political economy of trust."

Although I focus on the key structural dynamics and the systemic logic of contemporary capitalism, my analysis remains rooted in historical specificity: indeed, the social world is accumulated history. I will abstain from saying more here about my take on capitalism's transmutations. Let me assure the reader, however, that despite my drawing earlier on Jacques Derrida's sagacity about the use and abuse of discourses of crisis, there won't be a need to put up a sign that says "Beware! Deconstruction Ahead!"[4]

1

THE CRISIS OF
CAPITALISM, ALMOST

*The crisis consists precisely in the fact that the old is dying and
the new cannot be born; in this interregnum a great variety of
morbid symptoms appear.*

— Antonio Gramsci, *Prison Notebooks* (1929–1935)

"CAPITALISM IS OVER" IS NO MORE

"A deftly timed call for the overthrow of capitalism," a *Financial
Times* reviewer wrote of David Harvey's book *The Enigma of Capital and the Crises of Capitalism* in the spring of 2010. "If this is
not a revolutionary moment what would be?" Forget about the
angry streets—the global Occupy movements, the Indignados
in Spain, the Greek insurgency against austerity politics that
lifted the Communist party Syriza to power. It was the very
intellectual bastion of capitalism that proclaimed its downfall in
the aftermath of the global financial meltdown.

Capitalism is, of course, always in some sort of trouble—crises
are essential to its operation, as both its critic Karl Marx and
its proponent Joseph Schumpeter would remind us.[1] It was
only with the final triumph of neoclassical economics in the late

twentieth century that the benevolent invisible hand of the market became an orthodoxy. The authority of neoliberal capitalism came to be built upon a ruling conception of the market's securing optimal outcomes "without error, instability, or crisis" (Shaikh 2016). However, the financial meltdown in the first decade of the twenty-first century stirred up pronouncements about the *terminal* crisis of capitalism—capitalism on its deathbed.

The banking crisis of 2007–2008 spurred a series of further crises: one of public finances, one of the real economy, and eventually, through rising unemployment, a social crisis. Moreover, as David Harvey has again reminded us, capitalism seems to be working ever harder to dig its own grave. Some of its less "creative contradictions"—its drive to accumulate capital beyond the means of investing it (as companies are sitting on cash), its penchant for reducing salaries and depriving consumers of their means of consumption, its compulsion to exploit nature to the point of extinction—seem to point, now more ominously than ever, to capitalism's impending doom (Harvey 2014). Social scientists and pundits have had much to say on the subject. Published in the aftermath of the financial breakdown, Paul Mattick's *Business as Usual: The Economic Crisis and the Failure of Capitalism* (2011) countered popular views that laid the blame for the crisis on human greed, strategic mistakes, and mismanagement—a position implying that, should these flaws of morality and behavior be corrected, the system will be fixed. The system, he vigorously argued, is unfixable.[2] Similarly, Wolfgang Streeck has claimed that under the pressures of declining growth, oligarchy, starvation of the public sphere, corruption, and international anarchy, the capitalist system is in terminal decline and can do nothing more than delay its ultimate demise. Governments are merely buying time through redistribution, financial regulation, and other policies that help create the illusion of wealth (Streeck 2014, 2016). Updating ecosocialism's longstanding position, Saral Sarkar asserts in *The Crises of Capitalism: A Different Study of Political Economy* (2014) that capitalism has finally reached its limits, because even in our age of "nonmaterial" information technology, capitalism still relies on resources soon to be used up. Paul Mason argues in his *PostCapitalism* (2015) that, as resilient as capitalism might be, it cannot survive the combined existential threats of an aging population in the Global North, a global debt crisis, and climate change. Moreover, he contends, we are about to effectively exit capitalism altogether, as information technologies contain not just a transformative potential (which can go in any direction), but a truly emancipatory force, fostering the development of a more socially just and sustainable economy. Slavoj Žižek (2018) insists that global capitalism is on the verge of vanishing entirely under the unbearable lightness of the automation of work, the rise of immaterial/intellectual labor, the virtualization of money, and the dissolving of class communities.

Overall, the diagnoses of capitalism's impending demise typically rely on three assertions. First, the system is about to collapse because of poor economic performance, including the exhaustion of the natural resources on which it draws. Second, the institutions on which it depends, namely those of liberal democracy, are giving in. Third, capitalism is losing its legitimacy as broader public support for it wanes. None of this has come to pass, or is about to pass. More importantly still, such a terminal crisis of capitalism is not a precondition for its overcoming. For now, let us remain with sketching the current predicament as an entry to this analysis.

It is worth noting that the admonitions about capitalism and the warnings of its demise that proliferated in the aftermath of the financial crisis did not come only from the Left. Pope Francis's public endorsement of Marx's critique of alienation and exploitation springs to mind, as does the 2009 image of French president Nicolas Sarkozy ostentatiously holding a copy of *Das Kapital*. Some of these pronouncements came from the business community itself. "Capitalism is dead," wrote Alec Reed, founder of one of the UK's largest private businesses (Reed 2011). In her speech at the 2014 Conference on Inclusive Capitalism, International Monetary Fund director Christine Lagarde spoke of financial capitalism's recent excesses, claiming, "One of the main casualties has been trust—in leaders, in institutions, in the free-market system itself" (Lagarde 2015). This intimated a crisis of the social system rather than just a financial and economic meltdown.

A decade after the crisis peaked, the economic engine of capitalism is still experiencing some difficulty and there is a general sense that much is amiss. Even as the economy is recovering, society is not: for most people, the recovery feels like a depression. The world economy is still in tatters. Societies have been crippled by financial volatility and meager growth. Employment is increasingly precarious for both rich and poor. Intensifying work pressures take a growing psychological toll even on the labor market "insiders" we so envy. The young are rightly anxious that they may never find a job. Given the proliferation of excellent grounds for massive discontent, the search for an alternative socioeconomic system, one that can deliver prosperity and justice, should be now taking a palpable shape. Instead, calls for the overthrow of capitalism have vanished. We have entered the zone of what Jacques Derrida (1983, 71) named the "crisis of crisis"—a situation when, even as the word "crisis" has deserted our vocabulary, the idea that the present world is in crisis persists.

As I find that the term "crisis of crisis" befits our current predicament, I will appropriate it and give it the following meaning.

A crisis is a brief moment of extreme challenge that marks a turning point in an entity's existence. There are, in principle, three solutions to a crisis: death, returning to the precrisis situation, or transitioning to a new state. The world is in a very peculiar historical conjuncture where none of these three options apply. Strategies for coping with the Great Recession (which will be addressed in chapter 5) have not solved the crisis. A state of chronic inflammation has set in, and short-term crisis management has become a new normal. Capitalism is not on the edge of its collapse, but it is surely on edge.

Calls for overthrowing capitalism have been replaced by calls for equality. Shortly after economist Robert Shiller received the Nobel Prize in 2013, he declared that "rising inequality in the United States and elsewhere in the world" was the most important problem faced by society (Shiller 2013). "Tax the Rich" became a rallying cry emanating from a series of widely discussed works on inequality, among them Thomas Piketty's *Capital in the Twenty-First Century* (2013) and *The Economics of Inequality* (2015), Anthony Atkinson's *Inequality: What Can Be Done?* (2015), Harry G. Frankfurt's *On Inequality* (2015), and Joseph E. Stiglitz's *The Price of Inequality* (2013) and *The Great Divide: Unequal Societies and What We Can Do about Them* (2015). To this is added the voice of IMF managing director Christine Lagarde, who has called (2017) for rising inequality to be urgently countered, as it is detrimental to sustainable growth. In the run-up to the May 2019 elections for the European Parliament, the Party of European Socialists adopted eight resolutions for equal society as a basis of its electoral platform.[3]

Aptly capturing the change of public mood, San Francisco artist Megan Wilson, who had drawn the famous mural *Capitalism Is Over* in Clarion Alley in 2011 (figure 1.1), replaced it with *Tax the Rich* in 2015 (figure 1.2).

FIGURE 1.1 Megan Wilson at work in San Francisco's Clarion Alley in 2011. (Published with the artist's permission.)

What happened to the prophesied, dreaded, anticipated crisis of capitalism? What has deflated the inspired calls to end it into the familiar, somewhat nagging calls to tax the rich? The latter action would indeed alleviate our frustration, might end social privilege and help reduce the deficits of public budgets, but it would not miraculously create a political economy that supplies livelihoods without harming nature and people. To understand why this discursive shift is so aberrant, precisely when

FIGURE 1.2 Megan Wilson at work in San Francisco's Clarion Alley in 2015. (Published with the artist's permission.)

capitalism's prospects have never been gloomier, let us consider two paradoxes present in the current situation.

CAPITALISM ON ITS DEATHBED: TWO PARADOXES

There has been a general agreement in policy and academic circles that the early twenty-first-century economic crisis was caused by neoliberal policies: that deregulation and liberalization of financial, product, and labor markets generated economic and social risks on an unmanageable scale. And yet, with slight variations in the United States and Europe, the remedy administered for the illness is precisely what caused it: deregulation, privatization, tax cuts, and budgetary austerity, all of which entail cuts to public investment and wages. Some palliative measures have been administered, among them protection of specific industries and raising the minimum wage. However, these do not present a coherent alternative to the policy set that caused and perpetuated the economic crisis. Many experts forewarn that another slump is in the offing.[4] Thus, even as capitalism emerges unscathed from its latest crisis, most of us have ended up both poorer and with more unstable sources of livelihood.

A powerful countermovement against the free market took shape in a similar context a century ago. Social historian Karl Polanyi noted at the time that the mobilization to protect society from the market was a broad societal endeavor because a wide range of vital social interests had been harmed by the unbridled market mechanism. As he writes, exactly "because not the economic but the social interests of different cross sections of the population were threatened by the market, persons belonging to various economic strata unconsciously joined forces to meet the danger." This consensus was brought about not by the threat the market economy represented to the interests of a particular social group, but because the market, disembedded from society, "became a threat to the human and natural components of the social fabric." This engendered a broad, cross-ideological coalition of forces—socialist and conservative parties, as well as the Catholic Church in Europe, which began mobilizing to protect society from the market (Polanyi 1944, 150, 154–55). Meanwhile, in the United States, the Social Christian movement among Protestants (the *Social Gospel*) was recruiting policy support against "competition, individualism, and self-interest as morally and ethically wayward, and call[ing] for a new society of cooperation, sharing and self-sacrifice" (Greenberg 1974, 16).

This consensus born at the dawn of the twentieth century persisted through most of it. The New Deal policies in the United States were enacted in the 1930s by a coalition of Democrats and the liberal wing of the Republican Party, a partnership that lasted until the late 1960s. During his 1964 presidential campaign, Lyndon B. Johnson promised a Great Society to end poverty in America and won a larger majority of the richest 5 percent of voters than did Hillary Clinton in 2016. By contrast, the twenty-first-century populist outrage against neoliberalism has propelled to power adepts of the free market in the United States and Britain, calling for the protection of "our" national capitalism from global capitalism. Adherents of the free market have thus stabilized their rule or been freshly inaugurated into public office despite, and often through, populist mobilizations.[5] Even though economic and financial crises have clearly brought about a social crisis, there have been no traces of a cross-ideological countermovement against the free market. The calls for income redistribution pale in comparison to the powerful wave that inaugurated and maintained the post–WWII welfare state.

Some one hundred years after the events Polanyi recorded, history is repeating itself, yet again as tragedy, as narrated in Matthew Desmond's graphic depiction of extreme poverty in the United States. In *Evicted: Poverty and Profit in the American City* (2016), he paints a life-size canvas of exploitative landlords and tenants living on the brink of homelessness in what is purported to be the richest market democracy in the world. In the wealthiest country on earth, 50 million people (out of around 320 million) live below the poverty line, and one in eight people struggle with hunger, on the verge of a destitution that mirrors that of nineteenth-century Britain or the 1930s Dust Bowl victims portrayed in John Steinbeck's *The Grapes of Wrath*.[6]

Yet the policy responses in our times of crisis have been strikingly different from those of a century ago. Back in the early twentieth century, socialist and conservative political elites came to a consensus that enabled the construction of postwar social capitalism and the welfare state, not only via income redistribution, but also by way of stabilization of employment contracts and the improvement of working conditions. By contrast, governments today, irrespective of their ideological allegiance, are running to the rescue of financial capital and big business and implementing austerity programs to reassure capital markets, at the social cost of growing poverty and precarity.

The first paradox of the missing crisis of capitalism concerns the lack of a wide consensus among political and intellectual elites on the need to save society from the market. The second, more alarming paradox is the lack of serious effort on the part of society to protect itself. It is in agony, yet it is bearing its pains with astonishing equanimity. The months-long Yellow Vest protests across France in 2018 and 2019, which involved barricades, fires, and hand-to-hand fighting with police, are a reminder of what is missing in the rest of our societies. The economy is doing better; the people are not. And yet, apart from sporadic eruptions of street protests, most of which peter out quickly, and the growth of antiestablishment (populist) parties and movements, there is a general tacit acceptance of the situation: we are taking pride in being resilient. Over the past hundred years, the energies of protest have been gradually deflating from *revolution* to *reform*, *resistance*, and now *resilience*.

Despite the global upsurge of popular protest (which originated with the Occupy Wall Street movement in September 2011 in New York and focused on issues of inequality and austerity), the legitimacy of the system known as "democratic capitalism" is hardly in crisis. As one famous slogan of the Spanish Indignados proclaimed, "We are not against the system: the system is against us" (in other words, we want more inclusive capitalism, not its downfall). In the United States, the protest took the shape mainly of electoral support for a maverick presidential candidate from the economic establishment. The most radical and enduring eruptions of economic discontent in the decade following the 2008 financial crisis were by the Yellow Vests, who protested the rising costs of living. This movement has remained defensive and even conservative in its failure to articulate an ambitious vision for societal reform akin to the 1968 revolution. The very protests against the neoliberal establishment contain signs of the enduring legitimacy of capitalism, even as it has been failing as an engine of economic prosperity. If democratic elections are any indicator of prevailing preferences in our societies (and they surely are a better indicator than street protests), those held in the mature democracies of Europe at the nadir of the crisis suggest that neoliberal capitalism has considerable popular support. The majority vote went persistently to the economically liberal center-right parties advocating the very economic model that caused the meltdown of 2008–2011; parties of the Left were drastically marginalized.[7] By all evidence, as Alastair Roberts (2013) has put it, free market capitalism has learned to control dissent.

At the same time, social surveys indicate that a growing number of people across the capital-labor divide are frustrated with the intensified performance pressures and employment uncertainty the so-called structural adjustment policies have generated. These respondents declare that they would prefer a much better work-life balance, including discretionary time beyond family obligations, thus indicating a desire for autonomy from the productivist pressures of both the workplace and the family. (This development is discussed in more detail in chapter 4.) This resentment of job-related pressures combines with unprecedentedly broad awareness that the way we produce and live our lives is toxic for the environment and increases the risks of life-threatening natural disasters.

However, rather than seeking a radical alternative to the moribund system, people have channeled their social frustration in two directions. The first of these is hatred of the super-rich: the rage against the 1 percent obscures and seems to condone the injustice of inequalities within the 99 percent, including rampant poverty. The second channel is xenophobia, as demonstrated by the phenomenal rise of electoral support for anti-immigrant and anti-EU parties in Europe and the spectacular mobilization propelling Donald Trump to the U.S. presidency. Both forms of protest can be read as nostalgic gestures toward a more inclusive capitalism, rather than its rejection.

Given all the destitution that the recent economic crisis has created, calls for equality seem to be somewhat petty and falling short of the mark. As philosopher Harry Frankfurt remarks in *Inequality* (2015), our preoccupation with inequality is out of place. We should be instead concerned with poverty: the poor suffer because they don't have enough, not because others have more and some far too much. We are therefore morally obligated not to achieve equality or reduce inequality, but to eliminate poverty, urges Frankfurt. From this perspective, reading Danny Dorling's *Inequality and the 1%* (2015) feels like a guilty treat, indulging our envy of the obscenely rich. That to be born outside the 1 percent has a dramatic impact on our lives—from limiting education and employment prospects to reducing life expectancy and damaging our mental health—might seem implausible, but it is exactly what we are in the mood to hear.

Our pleasure turns guilty once we recall Frankfurt's retort: that the accumulation of obscene wealth is a curious phenomenon and the juxtaposition of vast wealth and poverty is offensive, but the real injustice is that of poverty, not inequality.

Yet how is it that inequality rather than the growth of poverty, on the one hand, and massive precariousness, on the other, is being politicized, that is, turned into a politically significant social concern? To understand the remarkable significance of the shift from a discourse of crisis and rejection of capitalism to one focused on inequality, we need instead to ask this: Why has inequality, which has always been a feature of market societies, suddenly become so disturbing, so much discussed? Or, as Harry Frankfurt presses us to ask, why do many people appear to be more distressed by the rich than by the poor? When so many other things have gone wrong in capitalist democracies (from ecological crisis to rise in suicide rates), even a dramatic increase in inequality should not be sufficient to place it at the center of public discontent. What is really at stake here?

One possible explanation lies in the power of capitalism itself. As David Harvey has put it, "the performance of capitalism over the last 200 years has been nothing short of astonishingly creative" (2010, 46). His inventory of capitalism's creativity—e.g., the way it keeps finding new ways to extract value when the old roads become blocked—spans the shift from agricultural capitalism to industrial capitalism, the service economy, and, most recently, the "credit economy." This is a useful reminder of the shrewd ability of capitalism's economic engine to reinvent itself through crises. Yet it does not answer our question: why we now plead so eagerly for equality within capitalism rather than its more substantial overhaul.

The most impressive way in which capitalism has demonstrated its creativity may well be this: even at the lowest point of its performance, it has generated novel support for itself. But why? I will bypass the facile answer of the "false consciousness" that prevents the masses from perceiving the true nature of their condition and will look elsewhere. For, while we have been busy debating its crisis, neoliberal capitalism has metamorphosed into a new form. The economic crisis of the early twenty-first century helped to consolidate this transformation, but it certainly did not trigger it. I therefore propose that, instead of pondering the crisis of capitalism, we account for capitalism's renewed consolidation, focusing our critique on the way this has engendered new forms of injustice and domination, a subject to which I turn in the following chapters.

2

CAPITALISM UNDER SCRUTINY

From Concept to Critique

The coincidence of the changing of circumstances and of human activity or self-changing can be conceived and rationally understood only as revolutionary practice.

—Karl Marx, *Theses on Feuerbach* (1845)

In one view, the insurgences on the streets and in the electoral booths in the decade that followed the 2007–2008 economic meltdown pronounced the end of the neoliberal hegemony. They amounted to a rejection of the policy consensus that had secured that hegemony—unregulated markets, free trade, and low taxation (Fraser 2017b; Grundy and Avery 2017). This is indeed a plausible view. However, I will venture an alternative one. I will argue that neoliberalism had already mutated into a new, more robust and resilient form by the end of the twentieth century—well before the economic crisis. The rise of social protest, in the particular shape it has taken in the global North, is consolidating this transformation. To understand why our societies are not making a significant, concerted effort to protect themselves (akin to the countermovement against the free market that propelled the welfare state), we need to understand the nature of this new, postneoliberal capitalism.

Before I proceed with this argument, let me disclose in some detail the logic of conceptualization and reasoning I will deploy. As mentioned in the introduction, this chapter is freestanding. Readers not much theoretically inclined should feel free to forgo it and refer, whenever needed, to the definitions of key concepts in the appendix.

In earlier works, I advanced elements of critique committed to a nonideal, negativistic conception of emancipation from oppression, one aspiring to diminish suffering rather than to obtain the just society—what Amy Allen has aptly named "emancipation without utopia" (Azmanova 2012b, 2012c; Allen 2015). Critical theory's aversion to utopian blueprints can be traced back to Marx's preference to seek a given social formation's potential for emancipation (e.g., capitalism's internal contradictions and crises, the formation of the revolutionary subject) rather than design the just society in the style of utopian socialism. Indeed, Marx offered no detailed account of a post-capitalist society. In his writing, far from being an elaborate social model, communism is the realization of democracy as spontaneous self-organization of the people. This minimalist articulation of the contours of a just society is typical for the Frankfurt School tradition of critical social theory. It is present, for instance, in Jürgen Habermas's idea of a public sphere and a lifeworld untainted by the instrumental logics of power and money (e.g., Habermas 1981)—a conception developed without a substantive elaboration of the just society.

From the perspective of this nonutopian notion of social criticism, I have contended that "the proper purpose of critique, and of political action guided by it, is emancipation, not justice" (Azmanova 2011c, 117). In what follows, I will articulate a formula of analysis that will serve a triple methodological purpose: to (1) advance a diagnosis of the social relations in capitalist democracies of the Global North in the early twenty-first century;

(2) perform a normative assessment of the grievances of injustice these relations generate; and (3) discern the emancipatory potential available within these societies.

TWELVE TENETS OF CRITICAL SOCIAL THEORY

The combined scholarship of authors belonging to the Frankfurt School tradition (the post-Marxian style of critique that was conceived at the Institute for Social Research at Goethe University Frankfurt in the interwar period) amounts to a comprehensive analysis of modernity and capitalism. The following core points—drawn from a fraction of the group's output—serve as a basis for elaborating my framework of critique of contemporary capitalism.

1. Justice as Emancipation

Analysis in the style of what Max Horkheimer (1937) defined as "critical theory" in contrast to traditional theory is guided by an emancipatory interest (improving the human condition), rather than confining itself to understanding and explanation. Furthermore, this emancipatory interest concerns not the realization of an ideal of a just society (the utopian telos I mentioned above), but reducing domination by alleviating oppression.[1] Thus, for Marx, eliminating the private property of the means of production is not a programmatic element in the blueprint of communism as the singular just society. It is, rather, a way of removing one of the main sources of injustice that industrial capitalism of the nineteenth century systematically engendered—worker exploitation. Putting an end to the private property of the means of production (but not of private/personal property altogether)[2] is a way of achieving emancipation from specific sources of domination, not securing absolute freedom. It is this commitment to emancipation as removing sources of oppression that puts a check on any penchant for utopian descriptions of a just social order and directs the inquiry toward available opportunities for a less unjust world.[3]

2. Immanency of Critique

Socially induced injustice and liberation from it (justice) make sense only from the internal perspective of the (social) subjects of that experience "on their own terms." It is in this sense that Theodor W. Adorno formulated the concept of "immanent critique." This is as opposed to "transcendent critique," one performed from an imaginary "independent" point of reference from which standards of justice are supplied a priori (Adorno [1966] 1973).[4] Thus, I posit that, despite their internal pluralism, modern liberal democracies are societies animated by a commitment to individual autonomy and equality of citizenship within collective self-determination. This overarching commitment provides the basic matrix for their self-understanding and assessment (what Adorno would call their "immanent truth"), notwithstanding conflicting interpretations of these ideas the inhabitants of these societies might have.

3. Enabling Conditions

Critical theory proceeds to articulate not the *features* of a just social order, but the *conditions* enabling such an order and the *processes* for attaining it. It seeks to discern what Horkheimer discussed as "the enabling conditions for successful realization" (*Gelingen von Vollzügen*) within the very constitution of social relations. In other words, our social environment must be appropriately structured to allow individual autonomy within collective self-determination. This is the role that the collectivization of the means of production plays in Marx: socialization of labor thus achieved would in turn enable the transformation of specialized and alienated labor into creative and individuated practice. Once the productivist pressures of the profit motive are eliminated, the space opens for creative, fulfilling work that also satisfies needs. Alternatively, Habermas discerns the possibility of emancipation in terms of conditions regarding morality, democracy, and law propitious to the free opinion and will formation of all citizens. The subjects emerging from these conditions of socialization are then capable of engaging in deliberations through which they agree on the particular features of an emancipated form of life. Rainer Forst's (2011) normative model of critique, centered on our basic "right to justification," views reason-giving and reason-taking as such an emancipatory process.

4. Social Practice

The key ontological unit for critical social theory is social practice: the "practical" or "sensuous human activity" through which people produce their existence (Marx [1845] 1969, theses I and V). The reality of human existence is not to be reduced to vulgar materiality; neither is the production of material life to be reduced to the economy in a narrow sense, as Marx and his intellectual partner Friedrich Engels make clear on a few occasions.[5] Production is to be understood broadly in the sense of *social production* of existence or society's reproduction (1959a, preface). The emphasis is on the relational nature of practice, in contrast to "action" or "activity."

In order to regain the original Marxian understanding of the economy as the ensemble of practices through which society produces its material circumstances, I treat economic activity itself as a social practice[6] while seeing all social interactions as composing an "economy of practices" rather than "economic practices." (The term "economy of practices," coined by Pierre Bourdieu [1986], refers to the multiplicity of mundane social interactions that form a continuum of intersubjective practices invariably imbued with power and containing their own ever-shifting action orientations.) This allows me to avoid reducing the economic dynamics of capitalism to the "economy" understood only as the production, distribution, and consumption of goods and services.[7]

5. Society as a Social System (System of Social Relations)

Marx contends that human essence should be grasped not as an "abstraction inherent in each single individual" (as the Natural Law tradition postulates), but instead as *social* essence, whose reality is the "ensemble of the social relations" (Marx [1845] 1969: thesis VI). Society is thus to be understood holistically as a system of social relations: it "does not consist of individuals, but expresses the sum of interrelations, the relations within which these individuals stand" (Marx [1857] 1973, 265). This understanding of the social neither as a composite of individuals nor in a collectivist manner (society as community), but as intersubjective practices within a structured system of social relations, sets critical theory apart from the philosophical traditions of liberal individualism and communitarianism.

6. The "Practical" Nature of Suffering

Analysis focused on empirical experiences of injustice as displayed in specific human suffering. If "[a]ll social life is essentially practical" (Marx [1845] 1969: thesis VIII), all suffered injustice is a practical experience. Centering attention on socially produced harm that is experienced as injustice is a strong common denominator in the writing of the first generation of Frankfurt School authors.[8] In the oft-quoted remark of Theodor Adorno, even though "we do not know what the correct thing would be, we know exactly, to be sure, what the false thing is"[9]— that is, we do not need to be certain of what is right to know that something is amiss. Initially it is the commitment to countering particular forms of suffering that turns the minimalist utopian elements present in Marx's vision of communism into a negativistic formula of critique aimed at diminishing domination. Specific (claimed or proven) instances of suffering and oppression serve as empirical points of entry into the society that is the object of immanent critique. Importantly, claims do not automatically offer a normative guideline, a standard of justice. The privileged normative position of the victim is typical of American progressive politics: it has arisen out of the rights discourse associated with movements for civil rights, women's empowerment, and the rights of sexual minorities. However, this unduly narrows the scope of political claims both in terms of valid claimants (e.g., victims) and valid requests for justice to alleviate the suffering (Brown 1995; Dean 2009). Within a critical theory perspective, experiences of injustice are only an entry point for an analysis of the larger social dynamics at work (see tenet 8 below).

However, I will make two adjustments to this position. While every grievance could be used as an entry point for critique (e.g., bankers complaining about reduced bonuses), certain grievances have a higher heuristic potency—namely those that are perceived as a significant social pathology within the society being analyzed. Émile Durkheim, for example, used increased suicide rates as such an empirical entry point in elaborating his theory of social derangement (*anomie*). The broadly shared perceptions of a phenomenon as being a social pathology suggest that something is amiss, thus offering a disclosure of the structural contradictions (antinomies) that are at the roots of suffering (see tenet 12 below).[10]

7. *The Social Nature of Suffering*

Expressions of discontent and claims to suffered injustice are not to be taken at face value: they are viewed as symptoms of larger dynamics at work. As Nancy Fraser has noted, the empirical reference point of critical theory is to be grasped not so much in terms of individual and prepolitical (psychological) experiences of suffering, but ones related to social subordination (Fraser 2003, 205).

8. *Systemic Roots of Injustice*

The emancipatory vigor of critique does not stem from its voicing condemnation of those practices that engender suffering (as articulated in, say, civil society mobilizations against various forms of discrimination) by assessing these grievances against an abstract set of rights or norms of human dignity—the style of critique performed by liberal normative theory. Critical theory is not necessarily averse to this. However, social critique as conceived initially within the Frankfurt School has a different ambition, namely to bring to light the nature of the system of social relations generating suffering, whether or not expressed in claims to justice. When Marx states that "the standpoint of the old materialism is civil society; the standpoint of the new is human society or social humanity" (Marx [1845] 1969: thesis X), he thus discerns novel paths of normative critique, social criticism, and political action. Identifying the roots of injustice in terms of peculiarities of the social system paves the road to *social* transformation rather than simple *political* reform by erecting edifices against abuse (such as constitutional protections of basic rights), as liberal theory would prescribe.

This attention to the pattern of social relations at the root of suffering also distances critical social theory from the tradition of American pragmatism, even as both schools of thought share a preference for addressing historical forms of injustice rather than spelling out abstract principles of justice. Richard Rorty compares the liberal and the pragmatic approach in this way: "The difference between an appeal to end suffering and an appeal to rights is the difference between an appeal to fraternity, to fellow-feeling, to sympathetic concern, and an appeal to something that exists quite independently from anybody's feeling about anything—something that issues unconditional commands" (Rorty 1996, 15). In a similar manner, we could assert that the difference between an appeal to end suffering and an appeal for an overhaul of the social system is the difference between an appeal to fraternity, to fellow-feeling, to sympathetic concern—in a word, to a charitable attitude—and an appeal to make suffering impossible by altering the social conditions that engender that suffering in the first place.

9. Attention to Political Economy

A key feature of Marxian social analysis is attention to the social dynamics and structures that configure the distribution of power.

A source of social injustice is the particular for a given society's system of social relations, including the structure of the political economy within which the process of social reproduction takes place (Horkheimer 1937, 237). For the first generation of Frankfurt School authors, "political economy was the ultimate object and terrain of the critical enterprise," a position they inherited from Karl Marx and Georg Lukács (Arato 1982, 6). Even as it uses particular experiences of injustice as an empirical entry point for analysis, critical theory does not limit itself to addressing distinct grievances of suffering, but traces these to their roots in the mechanisms underlying the distribution of social advantage and disadvantage. In the original Marxian analysis, the institutionalized norm of the private property of the means of production structures social relations and results in the uneven distribution of power between the social classes of wage laborers and capital owners, as well as in the diminished capacity of society to pursue collective goals. The elimination of this norm is therefore a tool of emancipation. Later, the first generation of Frankfurt School authors directed attention to the political economy of consumerism in the twentieth century—to the dynamics of needs-creation through which capitalism expanded and penetrated everyday life. Emancipation therefore stands as a matter of eliminating not just specific *practices* causing suffering (such as poor remuneration or excessive consumption), but the very *sociostructural sources* of that suffering.

10. Capitalism as a Social Formation

The sociostructural sources of suffering (e.g., the processes of exploitation, alienation, misrecognition, and political and social exclusion) are to be analyzed within a larger critique of capitalism as a social formation typical of a society of commodity producers. Here, critical theory of Frankfurt School descent has evolved gradually in a direction from which I choose to deviate. Marx treats capitalism as a *comprehensive* system of social relations (see tenet 5 above), structured so as to serve the imperative of capital accumulation. The first generation of Frankfurt School authors preserves this comprehensive ontology of capitalism. In his analysis of capitalism, Adorno often refers to it as the "social whole" and "social totality," which is internally structured (e.g., Adorno 1973, 37, 47).[11] However, treating capitalism as a social system does not imply that there is no social life outside of capitalism's penchant for the pursuit of profit. The gradual overtaking of society by the dynamic of capital accumulation is a historical process. As Schumpeter notes, "The capitalist process slowly socializes economic life and much besides, this spells transformation of the whole of the social organism all parts of which are equally affected" (1943, 310).

In a radical departure from Marx, under the influence of structural functionalism, Habermas (1973) reworks the original idea of society as a system of structured social relations into a unity of functionally distinct and relatively autonomous economic, administrative, sociocultural, and legitimation systems or subsystems of action, each of which contributes to social integration. He presents the state and the market as distinct spheres of action, each with its own rationalities committed to, respectively, political/administrative efficiency and economic efficiency. Thus, while Marx perceives capitalism as a *social system* integrated through the overarching imperative of capital accumulation (with its concomitant dynamics of commodification, exploitation, and alienation), Habermas reduces its dynamics to the functioning of the market as one subsystem alongside others.

In my own analysis of the contemporary transformation of capitalism, I will revert to the original holistic understanding of capitalism as a comprehensive system of social relations, even as

I abandon the structure-superstructure dichotomy Marx employed to describe the relation of political rule to socioeconomic processes.[12] Conceptualizing capitalism as a system of social relations distances my approach from structural functionalism, which has become the dominant approach in the analyses of systems. The latter views society as an organism whose vital functions are performed by the market, the government, law, education, and other specialized structures as autonomous mechanisms ensuring social integration in their respective fields of operation. This view is markedly different from the Marxian understanding I endorse of society as a system of structured and institutionalized social relations, enacted through everyday practices (see tenet 4 above).[13]

II. Historicity

The particular autonomy-enabling conditions that critical theory aspires to discern have historical and contextual specificity that an abstract critique of capitalism cannot capture successfully. According to this requirement for historicity, we must start where we happen to be historically and culturally, from a particular kind of frustration or suffering experienced by human agents in their attempt to realize some historically specific project of a good life (Geuss 1981, 63). Successive generations of Frankfurt School authors have targeted the particular types of capitalism they witnessed, maintaining commitment to immanent critique and historicist accounts of injustice. The first generation focused on the emergence of state-managed ("late" or "advanced") capitalism; the second (e.g., Jürgen Habermas and Claus Offe) elaborated on its consolidated stage. After an unfortunate spell of silence in the 1980s and 1990s—the (not so) golden age of neoliberal capitalism—scrutiny of the political economy of contemporary capitalism has been revived for the twenty-first century.[14]

12. Antinomies

A feature of immanent critique that is present as much as in Marx's structural analysis of capitalism as in Adorno's moral philosophy is the critic's interest in those antinomies (tensions, contradictions) that are constitutive of a given historical form of social relations. Empirical experiences of suffering attain the status of social injustice in relation to their origination from the key antinomies latent in the constitution of the social order. These antinomies are both sources of suffering and emancipatory openings toward attainable possibilities for a less unjust world.

This outline of what I deem twelve essential tenets of critical social theory is not meant to be a comprehensive and rigorous overview of the style of intellectual critique and the nature of social criticism developed within the Frankfurt School. Such an account is not necessary for the purposes of this book. I next proceed to make three adjustments to these components in order to address two issues: (1) peculiarities in the formation of a political common sense in terms other than ideology understood as "false consciousness" and (2) the societal resources for political mobilization toward subverting capitalism.

THREE ADJUSTMENTS

Revision 1: The Repertoire of Capitalism

Capitalism has been conceptualized as a system of social relations institutionalized in a multitude of historical variations.

These variations concern national models that have coexisted synchronically[15] as well as in a diachronic succession from its initial liberal (entrepreneurial) modality, consolidated in the course of the nineteenth century, to its current form. I do not propose to see these successive modalities as distinct "epochs," but rather as reconfigurations of a repertoire. I use the term "modality" rather than "model" here in order to highlight the fact that the historical forms of capitalism being discussed are varieties within a general formula. I reserve the term "institutionalized social order" to refer to the unity of a social system and a political system—e.g., the democratic capitalism of contemporary Western societies or the autocratic capitalism of current-day Russia and China.

In discerning the constitutive features of capitalism as an overarching repertoire, I draw on both Karl Marx and Max Weber. The repertoire of capitalism centers on its constitutive dynamic (and operative logic)—what Marx discusses as "capital accumulation" and Weber as the pursuit of "forever renewed profit by means of continuous, rational, capitalistic enterprise" (Marx [1867] 1965; Weber [1904–1905] 1992, 17). I will refer to this systemic dynamic of capitalism as the *competitive production of profit*. Both Marx and Weber address capitalism's three core principles: competition, the productivist nature of work (labor engaged in the production of commodities), and profit-making. However, they do not use, to my knowledge, the formulation "competitive profit production," which I find best captures the system-generating dynamic of capitalism.

Although Marx offers no systematic analysis of competition, in his treatment of capital accumulation it is "the inner nature of capital, its essential character" (Marx [1857] 1976, Notebook 4). Being the general form of economic interaction among actors, competition is thus capitalism's coordinating mechanism, and acts as a "coercive law" through which the logic of capital accumulation is imposed on individuals and the whole society (Marx [1857] 1973, Notebook 4; [1867] 1965, ch. 10 and 12; [1885] 1956; [1894] 1981, ch. 10 and 50).[16] Weber speaks of the *pursuit* of profit as defining the "spirit" of capitalism (akin to Marx's term "profit motive"). This indeed defines the personal action-orientations of those who engage in capitalistic enterprise. However, it is the effective *making of profit* through the production, exchange, and consumption of commodities (goods and services produced for market exchange) that constitutes capitalism as a viable system of social relations. Competitive profit production therefore constitutes capitalism as a social system in the sense that without it, this social system would not be capitalistic. That is why I will refer to it as capitalism's core systemic dynamic, its operative logic. The competitive profit production is accompanied by primitive accumulation of capital: the appropriation of what is to be deployed in the competitive pursuit of profit. As David Harvey has observed, this process does not just precede capitalism; it is an ongoing "accumulation by dispossession" (2003, 158). In the twenty-first century, this has taken the form of appropriation of consumers' personal data by internet companies. I prefer to use the term *primitive appropriation* to highlight the element of arrogating property that is to be deployed in the pursuit of profit, rather than simply accumulating wealth. While both competitive profit production and primitive appropriation are systemic dynamics—shaping capitalism as a system of social relations—the former is constitutive of capitalism while the latter is a secondary process, an enabling condition. (Not all factors contributing to the emergence of a phenomenon remain as its constitutive features.) In combination, the three principles of capitalism (to recall, the pursuit of *profit* through the *production* of commodities in *competition* among economic actors) shape the economic process as one of actively creating needs, which are then satisfied. The vertiginous dynamics of ever-inflating consumption and production perpetuate capitalism by subjecting human beings, their societies, and their natural environment to this process. Moreover, as the livelihoods and social status of all members are generated by this process, they become not only dependent on it but start to value it as the wellspring of their existence. The institutions of democratic representation and participation can be expected to give expression to this dependence, much as they can be used to question and challenge it.

Competition as a valid and validating procedure is present in the legitimation logics of both capitalism and liberal democracy. Merit proven in the course of competition allows capitalism, a social system activated by the dynamic of competitive pursuit of profit, to align with liberal democracy, a political system activated by the competitive pursuit of popular endorsement for contenders' acquisition of political office. Thus, the competitive pursuit of profit and of public office emerges as the operative logic of democratic capitalism as an institutionalized social order or sociopolitical system.

The systemic dynamics of capitalism are enacted in everyday social practices through which people enter into particular social relations (as owners or managers of capital, as wage laborers or self-employed, as producers and consumers, as educators and learners). These practices and relations are structured via core institutions: private property and management of the means of production, the "free" labor contract, and the market as a mechanism of commodity exchange and a primary mechanism of economic governance—that is, for the allocation of productive inputs and social surplus.[17] Capitalism cannot be equated with a market economy. Neither can the economic dynamics of capitalism be reduced to the production, exchange, and consumption of goods. This is the case because capital accumulation is driven by needs-creation (and therefore by perceived needs) rather than by the satisfaction of needs, a process with very strong ideational components related to perceptions of life-chances and social status.[18]

For the purposes of my investigation, it is important to steer away from the rather enigmatic way in which the "structural dynamics" of capitalism is usually discussed, with structures having the connotation of something that lies under the surface and stands beyond our grasp and control. This is why I prefer to disaggregate capitalism's systemic and structural dimensions. On the one hand, competitive profit production and primitive appropriation are, respectively, its primary and secondary systemic dynamics. On the other hand, these dynamics are enacted through institutions that serve as enabling structures. The institution of private property gives a distinct structure to capitalistic social relations, with its known distributive outcomes regarding material resources and social status. However, it is the engagement of *all actors* in the process of competitive production of profit that establishes the nature of the social system as properly capitalistic. Engels (1845, ch. 3) notes that "competition of the workers among themselves is the worst side of the present state of things in its effect upon the worker, the sharpest weapon against the proletariat in the hands of the bourgeoisie." In China, the absence until recently of private property of the means of production, or the lack of proper market mechanisms in the allocation of productive inputs and social surplus, did not prevent its being a capitalist country, with the state acting as an entrepreneur in the global economy. In a similar vein, should all property in currently capitalist countries be nationalized and held in common by the workers (as per calls of the radical Left), but used for the purposes of competitive profit production in the global economy, these societies would be no less capitalistic. Structuring institutions (e.g., the church, patriarchy, private property) determine how life-chances are distributed in society, but systemic logics determine what a life-chance is. In capitalist societies, the competitive production of profit shapes perceptions of successful life and accomplished self.

Distinguishing in this way between the systemic and structural dimensions of capitalism allows me not only to offer a critique of the political economy of contemporary capitalism not centered exclusively in social relations of class (as much of the current resurgence of interest in political economy tends to do), but also to pay due attention to the dynamics of competitive profit production. It is important to distinguish between systemic and structural aspects in the functioning of capitalism for one simple reason: even if we obtain a society in which the means of production and management are in public hands and all members are included and perfectly equal, this does not mean that the society would not be engaged in the competitive production of profit, with all the negative effect this has on human beings and their natural environment. This is why my appeal is to focus, above all, on systemic dynamics and make sure that our struggles against inequality and exclusion do not inadvertently reinforce the systemic logic of capitalism. As I will argue, important emancipatory energies are now emerging in relation to this systemic logic rather than to forms of ownership, class structures, and distributive outcomes.

Concomitant to the operative logic of capitalism is what Max Weber described as its "ethos"—a set of worldviews that orient behavior and give it the meaning of rational enterprise under individual initiative.[19] This does not imply that capitalism is the engine of rational thought. As Schumpeter (1943, 164) aptly observes, rationalism preceded the rise of the capitalist order and "all that capitalism did was to give an impulse and a particular bend to the process." This "bend" is the particular connotation of economic rationality as rational enterprise under individual initiative, whose benchmark of success is the effective generation of profit.

To sum up: As a system of social relations typical of a society of commodity producers, capitalism has a basic repertoire of constitutive features: two systemic dynamics, the constitutive dynamic of competitive production of profit and an enabling dynamic of primitive appropriation; key institutions with structuring function; and an ethos orienting actors' behavior and giving it the meaning of rational enterprise under individual initiative. To this can be added another constitutive element: a "legitimation matrix," on which I elaborate below.

Revision 2: On the Dynamics of Politicization

My second adjustment to the core tenets of critical theory regards the notion of legitimacy. In order to account for the process of politicization—the manner in which social experiences translate, selectively, into politically relevant matters demanding policy solutions—I use a cluster of concepts that allow me to trace the legitimacy relationship between public authority and citizens down to the broader dynamics of political meaning-formation. These dynamics define what democratic publics consider to be significant issues of justice.

Most narrowly defined, the legitimacy relationship between public authority and citizens is built around a set of ideas about the functions public authority is expected to perform for society, what Claus Offe has described as "legitimate and legitimacy-conferring functions of the state."[20] Citizens might expect public authority to protect private property, defend territorial integrity, and safeguard order, and therefore condition their obedience on the state's successful performance of these functions—let us call them " political deliverables." These functions are *legitimate* in the sense that their content is determined by what the public expects the state to do for society. At the same time, they are *legitimacy-conferring* because it is by force of the successful exercise of these functions that the state (or any public authority) gains legitimacy. I will refer to the set of these functions that define the relationship between public authority and citizens as a "legitimacy deal." This has two characteristics: (1) it is not fixed—it varies according to context and evolves historically; and (2) its content depends on what are held to be both *desirable* and *feasible* services public authority is to render society. If a certain function is not considered feasible (e.g., provision of a social safety net), it exits the legitimacy deal, even though it might still be considered a desirable feature of the social order.

What shapes the legitimacy deal? What are deemed to be legitimate functions of the state are not just embodiments of the system's interests or functional needs. Public authority's functions are articulated within a symbolic fabric of perceptions within which they are socially constructed as being legitimate and legitimacy-conferring. The legitimacy deal thus evolves from within shared views about overarching core values. I will refer to this broader normative framework as a "legitimation matrix" to highlight the legitimating framework's foundational role: the matrix is the mold within which an entity originates, develops, and is contained.

While the legitimacy deal secures the legitimacy of public authority and the political system by defining the relationship of the former to society, the legitimation matrix grounds the legitimacy of the whole *social order*, as it defines the core norms that give it significance and signification. The legitimation matrix spells out shared ideas of life-chances (notions of a successful life and an accomplished self) and their fair distribution in society. The legitimacy deal, however, specifies what public authority's functions are in relation to the formation and distribution of life-chances. The original legitimation matrix of democratic capitalism combined two ground rules. The first, pertaining to capitalism, stipulates that risks and opportunities be correlated (that is, that taking risks should be rewarded with opportunities for improved life-chances). The second, pertaining to liberal democracy, is that all members of society should have an equal say over the way in which life-chances are distributed—the principle of equality of citizenship, enacted via the mechanisms of political representation and participation. As my analysis unfolds in subsequent chapters, I will argue that a driving force in the transformation of capitalism has been the adjustments made to the legitimacy deal in order to safeguard the legitimation matrix.

The perceptions shaping the legitimation matrix and the legitimacy deal are akin to ideology understood as mental representations specific to a given era: "a set of shared beliefs, inscribed in institutions, bound up with actions, and hence anchored in reality" (Boltanski and Chiapello 1999, 3). However, the term *ideology* has become loaded with too many connotations, from political doctrine to nebulous values. I will instead refer to the normative orientations from which legitimacy is sourced with the Weberian term *ethos*. This term sets apart the action-orienting set of shared beliefs from a Marxian understanding of ideology as false consciousness. It also distances it from the reductionist interpretation of "rational interest" attributed to human beings in classical economics. In discussing modes of orientation of social action, Weber speaks of rational orientation to a system of individual ends as well as to an absolute value, in contrast to affectual orientation and habit. Moreover, he conceptualizes "interests" in terms of the way actors themselves are aware of them (Weber [1920] 1947, 115–18). Weber's notion of self-interest as articulated in *The Theory of Social and Economic Organization* refers to an action-orientation guided by the rationality of the particular social action within which perceptions of self-interest take place. This is akin to the notion of ethos he develops in *The Protestant Ethic and the Spirit of Capitalism* to conceptualize the ideational orientations composing the "spirit" of capitalism in terms of proving one's merit through work: a "rational," orientation, tangible proxy for which is the creation of profit (and not the accumulation of wealth).

When I discuss altering public attitudes to democratic capitalism in subsequent chapters, I will use "ethos" to speak of the ensemble of worldviews, including perceptions of interest, that orient behavior and endow it with social meaning. Ethos cannot be equated with ideology, rational interest, and ethical norms. In my usage, it connotes the cognitive and normative orientations regarding views about truth, appropriateness, and acceptability—a societal "common sense" or rationality. Within the ethos of modern democratic societies, for a person to claim decisional power for political or economic office on grounds that he or she is fated for such an office would be nonsensical. Similarly, claiming that a human being can be deprived of life without any justification would not only be considered inappropriate and unacceptable in most of these societies—it would be absurd. Therefore, such an idea would not even enter public debates: it stands beyond the common sense of our societies, beyond their ethos. Rational justification is the fulcrum of any modern ethos, present as much in modern democracies as in modern dictatorships. (Note that the latter would either hide the killing or offer some rational justification.) It is under the normative pressures of this overarching ethos that the legitimation matrix and the legitimacy deal of a social order take shape.

The triad of concepts—ethos, legitimation matrix, legitimacy deal—speak to different stages of the process in the course of which suffered injustice becomes politically thinkable as an issue of justice demanding the attention of public authority. Not all experiences of suffering are voiced as grievances. From those that are, only a limited set are recognized as matters relevant to politics and valid objects of policy. The selection of which social phenomena do gain visibility as public concerns and in turn are recognized as being politically relevant is framed by society's ethos, by shared notions of truth, appropriateness, and acceptability. However, it is a more narrow set of normative and cognitive orientations—those that make up the specific legitimation matrix (ideas of fair distribution of life-chances, as well as what constitutes a life chance)—that determine the thematic scope of the agenda of public debate: which social practices become politicized and thus objects of contestation and which ones are accepted as a matter of course and therefore remain unchallenged. This is a crucial point in my conceptualization of the missing crisis of capitalism (in chapter 5). To the extent that a certain type of social suffering is not politicized, there is no legitimation crisis of the socioeconomic and political order.

The dynamics of politicization are most often, but not exclusively triggered by acts of contestation, when particular experiences are articulated as grievances of suffered injustice, usually through civil society mobilizations. Collective perceptions of what issues count as salient shape the cognitive framework of reference within which public debates are articulated. In other words, the formulation of conflicting positions (e.g., for or against home schooling, for or against gun control) is enabled by a basic overlapping agreement on what counts in the first place as a set of significant social issues that can be an object of meaningful disagreement in the public sphere (Azmanova 2012b).[21] This process of contestation and public debate, in turn, generates a more specific "framework of political reference" that singles out some themes as politically relevant—that is, demanding policy action because they have to do with the fair distribution of life-chances in society as spelled out in the legitimation matrix. Social phenomena such as poverty, inequality, crime, and environmental degradation at some point enter the framework of political reference and gain a chance to be politicized into salient subject matter of political rule. Note, however, how the phenomenon of school shootings, even if it has become a highly important issue in public debates (that is, it has entered the framework of political relevance) has failed to be fully politicized into an object of public policy. In the course of such battles over the politicization of social concerns, a more concrete "legitimacy deal" eventually emerges—a deal spelling out the desirable and feasible political deliverables, actions public authority is expected to undertake in order to remain legitimate.

It is here, in my treatment of legitimacy and legitimation as a process of ongoing politicization spanning from mundane everyday interactions through contestations of the existing order and eventually to policies, that I depart significantly from Jürgen Habermas's take on legitimacy in his analysis of the legitimation of capitalism. His approach rests on two fundamental assumptions missing in my analysis. The first is that there exists a clear-cut divide between, on one hand, the systems of economic production and political administration and, on the other, the lifeworld of our social togetherness. These two distinct planes of our collective existence contain incompatible action orientations toward success or mutual understanding, respectively

(Habermas 1981). Instead, I perceive the fabric of social interactions in terms of interwoven practices that permeate all spheres of life, and whose significance and signification (in the eyes of participants) is secured by a shared societal ethos.

The second assumption I do not take over from Habermas's treatment is that a system's legitimacy is something set, a constant that varies only quantitatively. His belief is that we can speak of degrees of legitimacy—that is, there is, in principle, a limit to the penetration of the instrumental rationality of the economic and political systems of democratic capitalism into the lifeworld, beyond which problems of social integration ensue and the systems become beset by legitimation crisis. Even as I endorse this position as a normative ideal (that is, that the vision of a lifeworld free of considerations of efficiency is a good thing to strive for), I cannot endorse it as a reliable ontological model of the social order. Instead, I regard the process of legitimation as a dynamic one: which social phenomena are articulated as features of an acceptable socioeconomic and political order is entirely a matter of their politicization. This takes place within a frame of political reference that spells out issues considered salient for public debate and the desirable and feasible functions of public authority (i.e., the legitimacy deal) in reference to the fair distribution of life-chances in society as spelled out within the basic legitimation matrix.

The perpetually evolving framework of political reference mediates between the distribution of life-chances in society and policy action. This process begins with civil society's mobilizations in articulating and giving public visibility to systematic occurrences of injustice such as the disproportional power of the wealthiest 1 percent (the Occupy movements), unemployment among the young (the Indignados), complicity between corporate and political elites (the Tea Party movement), or gun ownership (the protests following mass shootings in U.S. schools). This articulation by civil society of concerns with injustice incessantly alters the framework of reference for public debates on justice. In a properly functioning democracy, the channel between civil society and political society (i.e., parties and political institutions) is open. This allows the process of politicization to take place as concerns raised by citizens about injustice are translated as policy issues by political actors struggling to gain public office. In this sense, it is wrong to blame civil society for its failure to affect politics. The job of civil society is to render certain experiences of injustice visible, salient issues of public concern—that is, to politicize them into claims to justice—and thus alter the framework of political reference. The fact that there is no political intake of these concerns into public policy, that political society has become impervious to some forms of grievances voiced by civil society, is a phenomenon to be scrutinized carefully, as we will do in chapter 5. This has much to tell us about the current state of capitalist democracies.

Revision 3: Forms of Domination and Types of Injustice

The third adjustment I introduce concerns the patterns of injustice that are objects of critique.[22] I specified earlier that I regard capitalism as a social system with constitutive and enabling dynamics enacted with the help of institutions with structuring effect, which in turn affect the distribution of life-chances in society. It will be useful to delineate specific trajectories along which experiences of injustice emerge in order to make their patterns distinct objects of critique. I propose to discern these patterns by focusing attention on the main forms of domination characteristic of capitalism, namely:

(a) *Relational domination*: This involves the subordination of one group of actors to another by force of the unequal distribution of power in society. The power asymmetries result from the unequal distribution of material or ideational resources (e.g., wealth, knowledge, recognition). Typical forms of injustice on the plane of relational domination are inequalities and exclusion. To remedy them, it suffices to equalize the distribution of power by, say, policies of wealth redistribution and political and cultural inclusion. Political theory that perceives power in agential terms tends to focus attention exclusively on these types of injustice. I do not claim that every inequality of resources generates domination; I am suggesting that there are forms of domination that can be traced back to power asymmetries resulting from unequal distribution of resources. (The rich may not dominate and the dominators may not be rich, yet the rich may have systematic undue influence by force of their superior resources, under certain conditions that need to be explored.)[23]

(b) *Systemic domination*: This form of domination subordinates all members of society to the constitutive dynamic of the social system; they shape their lives according to it and internalize its operative logic in the form of understanding of social and personal achievement and self-worth. Both the winners and the losers in the asymmetrical distribution of power are subjected to systemic domination. In the case of capitalism, systemic domination is engendered predominantly by the imperative of competitive production of profit. The owners and managers of capital as well as the workers succumb to this imperative. Here, injustice has to do with social harm beyond the unequal distribution of social advantage and disadvantage: it is engendered by the very notion of what counts as social advantage, itself shaped by the constitutive dynamic of the system. In other words, a valid source of suffering on this plane of injustice is not the unequal distribution of social status, but the system-specific definition of social status. The object of critique is therefore not the way power resources (wealth, political office, respect) are distributed, but what counts as a resource and how this resource is valued as a desired good. We ask not who is excluded from a form of well-being, but how notions of well-being are constituted and enacted in social practices.

Marx introduced this trajectory of domination in his analyses of alienation (the multifaceted estrangement of people from their humanity, their "species-essence"). Although he focused predominantly on the effect of alienation on wage labor, there is no reason to claim that the impact of the competitive production of profit is not suffered by all members of a society of commodity producers. The alienation thesis therefore applies to all participants in this process: the profit motive permeates all spheres of human existence, resulting in a broad spectrum of suffered injustice. (This view is implicit in, for instance, Habermas's thesis of the "colonization of the lifeworld."[24]) The inventory of such socially induced suffering spans the intensified productivist pressures that prevent a fulfilling or even healthy work-life balance, the increased health hazards as companies prioritize profit over safety, and the destruction of our natural environment. In the case of democracy as a political system animated by an overarching commitment to popular sovereignty, systemic injustice comprises giving priority to the immediate interests of a particular national community over the interests of future generations, humanity as a whole, and the natural environment. Policies of equality (such as rising wages) and inclusion (expansion of the electoral franchise) would not suffice to counter the harms of systemic domination.

(c) *Structural domination*: This form of domination concerns the constraints on judgment and action imposed on actors by the main structures of the social system, the institutions through which the operative logic of the system is enacted. In the case of capitalism as a social system, this concerns the structures of private property and management of the means of production, as well as the market as a mechanism of economic governance. In the case of democracy as a political system, the main structure is that of electoral competition and the electoral franchise, which together enact the systemic logic of the competitive pursuit of public office.

Structural injustice takes the form not of inequality and exclusion (the ambit of relational domination), but of the actors' incapacity to control the institutions through which the constitutive dynamic of the social system is enacted. This translates as their impotency to affect the "rules of the game" or alter the systemic logic. This is the case because their very integration into society depends on these structures, which in turn affects the actor's understanding of his or her short-term interest and political orientation.

Within the original Marxian analysis of capitalism, exploitation is the key structural injustice in this social system. The structure of the private property of the means of production, together with the nominally free labor contract, is what allows the exploitation of labor: it gives the owners the power to extract surplus value from their workers. Raising the living standards of the working class (returning to workers, in the form of higher wages or other benefits, a bigger share of the value they produce) would not terminate exploitation. Only eliminating class differentiation by way of abolishing the private property of the means of production would do so. However, note that this might not nec-essarily abate the competitive production of profit and its atten-dant alienation, as the experience of "real socialism" in Eastern Europe and elsewhere made clear. The particular social harm incurred by the market as a structure of commodity exchange is the commodification of labor and nature, i.e., treating human beings' creative capacities as well as our natural environment as goods "produced" exclusively for market exchange. In the case of democracy as a political system, the social harm incurred by the structures of electoral competition and the electoral franchise are the "privatization" of public life and the poor quality of pub-lic service.[25]

Disaggregating in this way the notion of domination along the above-described three dimensions allows us to cast the web of critique as broadly as possible, investigating (1) the injustice of oppression that powerful groups exercise over other groups and over society as class or group domination, (2) the structures through which they exercise this power, and (3) the systemic sources and systemic nature of that oppression, beyond the par-ticular groups who profit from the uneven distribution of power. This allows us to conceptualize the "oppressor" as a "complex sys-tem that combines persons, networks, and machines with no obvious centre," as Saskia Sassen (2014, 10) has put it. As the focus of the current analysis is capitalism, the conceptualization I offer will help to trace the seemingly nebulous power of that complex system to its constitutive dynamic—the competitive production of profit.[26]

Such a disaggregated understanding of domination is to help the analysis avoid two traps. On the one hand, critique of capi-talism that is cast narrowly in terms of class interests and group domination and traces these interests to the position of social actors vis-à-vis structuring institutions (i.e., the private property of the means of production) unduly limits the remit of criticism to the injustice of unequal distribution of social advantage. This perspective privileges the question "who dominates?" at the expense of the question "what dominates?" Introducing the notion of systemic domination allows us to acknowledge the social nature of the "rules of the game" and address injustices rooted in the very operative logic by force of which a social order is constituted. It prompts us to scrutinize not only the unjust stratification of life-chances but also to question what counts as a life-chance.

However, on its own, a critique of systemic domination that concerns itself with the social genesis of roles and rules risks presenting people's actions as an outcome of obeying rules beyond their control. Not only does such a totalizing notion of domination (one typical of structuralism and systems theory) force us to think of ourselves as being held captive by that system, but it risks exculpating perpetrators of injustice as themselves being innocent victims of the system.[27] The differentiated notion of domination I offer allows demystification of the nebulous structures and processes at work behind power dynamics, accounting for the injustice of the unequal distribution of power and holding to account those who profit from inequalities, while not remaining blind to or uncritical of the broader social dynamics that shape the system within which we seek equality and inclusion.

The three trajectories of domination are often in conflict. This presents a challenge for intellectual critique, social criticism, and political action that I call *the paradox of emancipation*. Social protest and intellectual critique are often triggered by tangible injustices in the realm of relational domination (inequalities and exclusion). However, the realm of relational domination is often the arena where victims fight other victims while the perpetrator runs free. For instance, feminist struggles for women's parity with men in the labor market have achieved a pyrrhic victory: in failing to reject the socioeconomic model within which women aspired to parity, they overlooked the systemic injustice of labor commodification and the increasing pressures for remaining competitive, employable, and employed. These harms are suffered by men as well (Fraser 2009; Azmanova 2012a, 2016a).

The problem goes even further. Successful struggles against inequality and exclusion and the structures that enable them do not simply obscure systemic domination: they often enhance it. This happens because such struggles confer value on the system (and the attendant notions of a successful life and an accomplished person) within which we seek equality and inclusion. In this way, struggles against relational and structural domination risk deepening systemic domination. While feminists struggled against the oppressive structure of patriarchy and fought for equality with men in the labor market, women in fact increased the desirability and, ergo, the legitimacy of the competitive production of profit as a systemic dynamic of capitalism. Struggles against global capitalism such as "America First" and Brexit valorize capitalism at home. The welfare state consensus on inclusive growth and redistribution has elevated the value of prosperity into a right to be middle-class, with expectations for ever-improving living standards. This formula of prosperity-for-all remedied the relational injustice of inequality, but did so to a great extent by deepening the systemic injustice of environmental destruction.

The protests of the Indignados against austerity policy expressed the paradox of emancipation perfectly in their famous slogan "We are not against the system; the system is against us." They render the system more valuable through calls for being included in it. This is how the validation of the system often penetrates the language of protest and disables the radicalization of social protest: that is, it prevents the transition from fighting relational forms of injustice to fighting systemic ones. That is why it is imperative that when addressing inequality and exclusion, intellectual critique and political mobilization make sure to also target the very constitutive logic of the social order within which inclusion and equality are being pursued.

This leads me to the final element of the theoretical model that guides my analysis: the notions of *emancipatory* and *radical* practices. I noted in tenet 4 that social practice is the main unit of analysis, referring to intersubjective action through which people both create their social reality and make sense of it. As Marx observed, herein lies the potential for radical emancipatory transformation, for "revolutionary" or "practical-critical" activity (Marx [1845] 1969, theses I and III). In light of the three forms of domination delineated above, I propose to define emancipatory social practices as ones that target these forms of domination. The term *radical practice*, however, I reserve for practices that aim to eradicate systemic domination. Successful radical change would therefore not necessitate a political revolution, a terminal crisis of capitalism, or a utopia to steer us toward transformation. Radical change would be a matter of mobilizing a broad coalition of social forces to engage in radical practices meant to eliminate injustices rooted in the systemic dynamics of capitalism, namely the competitive production of profit.

As to the vocation of intellectual critique, I have averred that the purpose of critique is not to spell out principles of justice or features of the good life, but to bring to light the sociostructural origin of experiences of injustice in order to articulate a path for emancipation by reducing oppression (Azmanova 2011c, 117; 2012b, 50–52, 228–36; 2012c). However, only by targeting systemic domination can there be radical change. To be truly radical, therefore, a critical theorist needs at minimum to identify and signal the danger of deepening systemic domination while fighting successfully other forms of domination—to alert against the "paradox of emancipation." The ultimate goal of the critical enterprise is to illuminate possible alliances (beyond animosities over the unfair distribution of resources and opportunities) that are capable of delivering such radical change.

It is time to attempt to put the above elements of analysis into a formula of critique and ask what it would mean to conduct a normative and diagnostic analysis of our contemporary social and political order from the perspective of critical social theory. Such analysis would proceed from a specific grievance, preferably one perceived largely as a social pathology, and use it as an empirical entry point. It would then trace the manner in which grievances of injustice, expressed by civil society, affect the framework of political reference by making these concerns politically salient in a particular way, namely, having to do with the fair distribution of life-chances as specified by the dominant legitimation matrix. It would scrutinize the terms in which grievances are politicized—that is, how they obtain political significance as claims to justice and appeals for policy action—and how they eventually alter the legitimacy deal between citizens and public authority.

Further, the inquiry would direct attention to the structural and systemic dynamics of the social order: the three forms of domination and patterns of injustice related to them. It would seek to identify those antinomies (contradictions) of contemporary capitalism that foster *historically particular*, but *structurally general* experiences of injustice from which *normatively generalizable* notions of justice can be derived.

Such an analysis should be guided by the following questions: What are the key dynamics at work within the political economy of contemporary capitalism? In other words, what are the drivers in the *formation* and *distribution* of life-chances in the globally integrated capitalism of the early twenty-first century? How do these dynamics trigger structural antinomies that in turn translate into historical patterns of social injustice within the trajectories of relational, structural, and systemic domination? What is the common denominator behind the various, often conflicting grievances? What places them in an agonistic dialogue of a meaningful disagreement about injustice? This will eventually allow us to derive normatively generalizable notions of justice that can guide progressive politics as strategies of emancipation befitting the historical circumstances of our times. These strategies will take shape as emancipatory practices that target relational, structural, and systemic forms of domination.

Let us now put this formula to work in a sociohistorical critique of present-day capitalism.

3

IDEOLOGIES FOR
THE NEW CENTURY

*The totalitarian world, whether founded on Marx, Islam, or
anything else, is a world of answers rather than questions.*
—Milan Kundera, *The Book of Laughter and Forgetting* (1979)

XENOPHOBIC COMMON SENSE

"We cannot take on the burden of all these desperate people,
Italy has its own problems . . . this is a battle for legality, social
justice, and freedom for our people," states Mariano Falcone, an
activist of Italy's far-right Northern League party in the port city
of Salerno, where ships dock carrying asylum-seekers. He speaks
of "attempted Islamization," the injustice of "ethnic substitution,"
and the likelihood of "ferocious social clashes" between poor
Italians and the growing immigrant population.[1] This anti-
immigration discourse engages all key terms in the familiar lexicon of justice: it invokes commitment to the rule of law, economic
fairness, social cohesion, freedom, and popular sovereignty
within a national community, seasoned with a humanistic com-
passion for the sorry fate of "these desperate people." But what
particular grievance does it express? What are the questions to
which this new brand of xenophobia offers an answer?

The procedure of critique I laid out in the previous chapter starts off from an empirical entry point: a grievance about suffered injustice, preferably a phenomenon that tends to be perceived as a pathology, as the tensions it exposes are likely to direct us to deeper social contradictions at the core of the social order. Let us take the rise of xenophobia in the affluent Global North as an empirical point of entry into these societies in their current condition. While the fear and hatred of foreigners is most vocally expressed by far-right parties and movements, anti-immigrant sentiment has also overtaken the political mainstream. Responding to the same resentments that precipitated Brexit, the leader of the British Labour Party launched the slogan "British jobs for British workers" a decade before the fateful referendum.[2] Expressing the public mood ahead of the March 2017 parliamentary elections in the Netherlands, Prime Minister Mark Rutte published a warning to immigrants, "Behave normally or leave the country!" Rutte is not a far-right politician: he leads the culturally and economically liberal center-right People's Party for Freedom and Democracy. The electoral rise of far-right parties has pushed xenophobia into mainstream politics. (It is all the more remarkable that some radical Left parties and movements, labeled "left populism," such as Syriza in Greece and Podemos in Spain, have steered clear of this noxious sentiment.)

One might see the growth of anti-immigrant attitudes as society's natural instinct for self-preservation from forces that overwhelm them. More than a million migrants crossed into Europe in 2015, triggering talk of an "immigration crisis"; another million followed in 2016, with asylum claims more than doubling from the previous year (EP 2017). Reportedly, this was the worst such disaster since World War II. Yet the comparison is poorly grounded in fact. Some sixty million Europeans became refugees during the World War II period. The population of the European Union numbered over five hundred million in 2016. Moreover, European societies now have the affluence and institutional know-how to absorb the newcomers. This is hardly a crisis. This discrepancy between the material capacity of Western societies to absorb newcomers and the growing public resentment toward immigration sharpens the sense of the pathological nature of the rise of xenophobia.

Among the many attempts to account for the upsurge of xenophobic attitudes in the West, Zygmunt Bauman has offered perhaps the most compelling one: "Refugees are strangers to us; and strangers are frightening because they are dangerous." Thus Bauman opened his public lecture at a gathering in Istanbul a few years ago as he introduced to the audience his new research for what later became the monograph *Strangers at Our Door* (2016).[3] By "strangers being dangerous," Bauman had in mind that they embody what Russian thinker Mikhail Bakhtin has called our "cosmic dread": the anxiety we experience in the face of the infinitely enormous and powerful forces beyond human control, fear that is at the very foundation of human experience and thinking. This fear is now exacerbated, Bauman noted, by the planetwide interdependence that marks the state of "liquid modernity"—a life in perpetual flux. As refugees bring to our door the distant horrors of global forces, we demonize them as harbingers of bad news.

Much as this diagnosis sounds plausible and intellectually elegant, it is not fully convincing. Although it acknowledges the destabilizing effect of globalization, it overlooks the sociopolitical conditions that enable strangeness to be experienced as threatening. As I was growing up under the policed safety of the dictatorship in my native Bulgaria, I lived in a world in which strangers knocking on your door were harbingers not of bad news, but of liberating novelty; they were certainly much less frightening than a policeman on the doorstep. Parting ways with Bauman, I will therefore take my inquiry away from the psychological anthropology of attitudes to strangers (without gainsaying the relevance of this perspective) and focus instead on the sociopolitical conditions that make the experience of strangers at our door a frightening one.

This is the approach that John Judis adopts in *The Populist Explosion: How the Great Recession Transformed American and European Politics* (2016). This analysis not only highlights the importance of the sense of physical fear generated by the September 11th attacks, but also places a welcome stress on the political economy, noting that technocratic elites lost credibility in the global financial crisis in 2008, triggering an outrage that found expression in both right-wing and left-wing antiestablishment mobilizations. And yet, one significant fact challenges this argument: the rise of both antiestablishment and antiforeigner sentiment (the two elements of the populist upsurge) had already begun at the close of the twentieth century, well before 9/11 and the economic meltdown. The combination of xenophobic and antiestablishment sentiment, as well as the context in which it emerged (both in terms of timing and location), provides clues to the peculiar nature of the most recent populist upsurge.

UNCOMMON POPULISM

It was during the affluent 1990s that old far-right parties such as the Front National in France and new formations such as the anti-Islamic but culturally liberal Lijst Pim Fortuyn movement in the Netherlands (the predecessor of the Partij voor de Vrijheid) gained popularity—in conditions of good economic growth, rising living standards, and low unemployment.[4] Such sentiment spread, in particular, in relatively rich and egalitarian countries such as Switzerland, France, the Netherlands, Sweden, and Finland. (At this time, Germany was experiencing an economic downturn, but no anti-immigrant mobilization emerged.) This marks a striking deviation from the past: the rise of xenophobia is commonly a consequence of societal breakdown in conditions of economic malaise and political turmoil, as in the growth of fascism and Nazism after World War I.

Another peculiarity of the antiforeigner upsurge merits attention: In the "classical" version of xenophobia propagated by far-right parties, hostility to foreigners was cast in terms of cultural superiority and political sovereignty (national chauvinism). By contrast, the new xenophobia is strongly economic in essence, notwithstanding the ethnoreligious terms in which it is voiced. Its first tangible expression in Europe was the mobilization, across the left–right divide, against the "Polish plumber" in France during the 2005 EU constitutional referendum, when people voiced fears that the influx of cheaper labor from the new member-states after the Union's Eastern enlargement would undercut wages and thereby trigger social dumping in the old ones.[5] This was symptomatic of the emergence of a novel agenda of public concerns (a new framework of political relevance) within which xenophobia gained its particular common sense. Indicative of this nascent framework was the split within the Italian Left at the 2008 general elections, caused by the espousal of an antiforeigner position on ownership and employment by Fausto Bertinotti, the leader of Communist Refoundation. He supported center-right prime minister Silvio Berlusconi's opposition to the takeover of Alitalia by Air France–KLM, implying that foreign competition was a greater enemy to Italy's workers than their bosses. This dovetailed with an argument made by the leader of the extreme-right Northern League, Umberto Bossi (Dinmore 2008). In the United States, participants in the Tea Party movement that was formed officially in 2009 (which cast itself as the party of Main Street against those "banker-bailing, crony-capitalist Obama Democrats") spoke of "illegal immigrants" as freeloaders who were allowed to drain the public coffers despite breaking the law.[6]

The novel nature of xenophobia is also signaled by a change in the policy preferences of far-right parties, the movement's standard-bearers. "Classical" parties of the Far Right, as well as most of its new formations, have abandoned their original endorsement of free markets and are now calling for social protection as well as closed-border policies. Their hostile stance to free and open markets has been recorded only since the late 1990s, first in the discourse of the founder of Le Front National, Jean-Marie Le Pen.[7] In the United States, the Tea Party movement has voiced support for raising the U.S. minimum wage while trying to steer away from traditional conservative issues such as prayer in schools, abortion, and gun control.

To this may be added the striking phenomenon that, in contrast to the traditionalism typical of the political Right, many of Europe's far-right xenophobic parties and movements have endorsed a culturally liberal agenda (e.g., gender equity and LGBTQ rights). Their narrative is that they are protecting Western liberalism from the traditonalist, conservative Muslim culture. The newly emerged "hipster right" or "Identitarian" movement—a mobilization of young, educated, technologically savvy people active in France, Austria, Italy, and Germany—is particularly illustrative of this merging of liberal values, concerns for economic justice, and xenophobic sentiment. In opposing immigration from Africa and the Middle East under slogans such as "Secure Borders Secure Futures," their discourse is ostensibly centered on cultural identity both in terms of national heritage and European liberal (but not cosmopolitan) values. However, it also features the prominent threat that "economic refugees" bring to Europeans' livelihood.[8]

These peculiarities invite us to search for an engine of anxiety beyond the alleged threats of Islamization and terrorism that have come to frame the xenophobic discourse. To this end, let us take our inquiry back to the context in which populist mobilizations first emerged: the closing decade of the twentieth century.

Two peculiarities of the socioeconomic landscape of the affluent 1990s merit attention. First, this was a time of intensive liberalization of the economy via deregulation of product and labor markets, coupled with an opening of national economies to the global market via free trade and investment. This combination became a core feature of neoliberal capitalism. It entailed a simultaneous thinning of the social safety net and intensification of competition. Second, this was a time of intensive development of information technology, which enabled the automation of a wide spectrum of economic activities beyond routine jobs. Center-left and center-right ruling elites came to pursue the creation of the knowledge economy of open borders, bringing about the era of what has come to be known as "globalization." Although the term is used as shorthand for the latest stage of global integration (and I will continue using it when describing public attitudes), it is misleading because global economic interdependence has a long history.[9] I will address the specific components of the current wave of globalization and their particular social significance in the next chapter. What is relevant to note in discussing the public sensitivities and grievances that concern us now is that in its dynamism, globalization has triggered

massive destabilization, which has been well recorded in scholarship on the risk society. Ulrich Beck (1992) has argued that
the very logic of advanced industrial societies has shifted from
wealth-production to risk-production. Firm-level volatility
among publicly listed companies (in terms of revenues, profitability, and employment) increased fourfold between 1960 and
2000 (Sull 2009). At the same time, the new economy of open
borders and technological upheaval has generated unprecedented
economic growth. Imports of cheap consumer goods raised the
purchasing power of Western societies, improving living standards and creating the impression of increased wealth.

However, even as these policies generated affluence, the combination of labor-market liberalization, automation of work,
and radical opening of national economies led to employment
insecurity and wage depression, fueling fears of (real, perceived,
and anticipated) loss of sources of livelihood. I stress here perceptions of current and future social status in reference to earning capacity, in line with economic studies affirming that people
make such judgments not as a matter of a rational choice calcu-
lation based on empirical circumstances, but at a deep psychological level (Friedman 2005). As fear of job outsourcing in the
context of globalization has been shared across the working and
middle classes, economic xenophobia has also tainted the discourse of the center left and the center right in Europe.[10] It is
the new economic nature of xenophobia that has allowed it to
enter the political mainstream.

The second feature of the context of the 1990s was that corruption and mismanagement scandals plagued the business and
political establishment. Trust in ruling elites plummeted, a development that preceded the economic meltdown of 2008.[11] The
combination of these two peculiarities—the destabilization
of the socioeconomic environment (despite growth) and the

discrediting of the establishment—allowed populist leaders in Europe to mobilize unprecedented support by alleging that ruling elites were reaping the benefits of growing prosperity, yet leaving society in ruins. Hostility to both central government and big business is shared by the far-right and radical-left formations in Europe. It also marks the stance of the Tea Party movement in the United States, whose hostility to corporate elites is all the more striking because billionaires, such as the founders of Koch Industries, are bankrolling it.

A pattern emerged around the turn of the twenty-first century: a protest vote expressing a frustration with economic uncertainty and with political elites' complacency, ineptitude, or sheer mendacity. This is evidenced also by studies revealing that the anti-austerity protests that erupted in the aftermath of the 2008 financial meltdown were not those of disappointed consumers. The indignation had to do not with austerity itself but rather with the *manner* in which it was imposed—as a result not of a cyclical economic crisis, but governments' bailing out of banks while cutting public spending. (European Union citizens bore the 2008–2011 bank bailout's €4.3 trillion cost.[12]) In this sense, the real grievance behind these protests was not impoverishment, but a feeling of unfair rule that privileges some economic actors at the expense of society. This frustration was indeed sharpened by the economic crisis, but was not generated by it.

What is being currently demonized in the mainstream media as "populism" can be seen, therefore, not as a transient expression of discontent, but as an expression of broadly shared and lasting anxiety triggered by perceptions of physical insecurity, political disorder, cultural estrangement, and employment insecurity resulting from employment flexibilization, job outsourcing, or competition with immigrants for jobs. These are the four ingredients of a new anti-precarity (order-and-security) public agenda.

Indicative of this shift is the way in which the issue of unemployment has begun to appear in political discourse. While the old paradigm is concerned with employment in terms of overall economic growth and efficiency, the new one addresses unemployment in terms of fear, loss, and marginalization.[13] This new set of public concerns emerged in the 1990s in conditions of continuous growth, low unemployment, and rising living standards. As this novel public agenda charts a new framework of reference for politics, it indicates that the ideological landscape of Western democracies is undergoing a remarkable transformation.

THE IDEOLOGICAL LANDSCAPE OF THE TWENTIETH CENTURY

In order to perceive the extent to which the ideological landscape of Western democracies has altered, it is useful to recall the contours of its basic structure as well as the role the mechanics of electoral politics play in aligning public demand with political supply of policies.

For most of their lifespan, liberal democracies have used a left–right divide to navigate the space of political meaning-formation and electoral competition. When this dichotomy first entered the vocabulary of politics in the eighteenth century, it signaled the emergence of two competing, but equally feasible paths for modern politics: keeping fidelity with a tradition (the conservative stance, on the right) or a radical break with it (the liberal stance, on the left).[14] In the course of the twentieth century, the conservative–liberal connotation of the left–right divide was, without being replaced, overlaid with opposing views regarding the manner through which society's economic welfare was to be achieved—via public authority's redistributive intervention (on the left) or the free market's unencumbered performance (on the right). The two familiar axes of modern ideological orientation emerged: an *economic* one, with preferences spanning from free market on the right to regulated market on the left, and a *cultural* one, with preferences spanning from traditional values on the right to liberal ones on the left.

While public demands and the politics on offer could, in principle, spread across the full spectrum of choices, it is the mechanism of electoral competition for voter support that has fostered the clustering of preferences along the two poles.[15] While two axes of ideological orientation serve to articulate diverse worldviews into politically meaningful positions (views on the economy, the role of government, the place of religion in public life, etc.), political dynamics are structured along a single axis. In terms of "political demand" by citizens, this axis aggregates the various *ideological positions* into contrasting *policy stances* (e.g., pro- or anti-abortion; for or against state regulation of financial markets). In terms of "political supply" (of policy ideas advanced by political actors), this axis directs the articulation of eligible *policy options*. The convergence of demand and supply underlies a viable representative democracy. The adjustment of party programs to public preferences grants legitimacy to the electoral process. Importantly, the dynamics of aligning supply and demand through electoral competition runs two ways: as parties are trying to discern the electorate's concerns and respond to them, they are also shaping that demand by way of providing the ideological language in which grievances are expressed.

In the famous "freezing of party systems" hypothesis that Seymour Martin Lipset and Stein Rokkan (1967) advanced some fifty years ago, the post-WWII party systems reflect the cleavage structures of the 1920s. In sum, the main distribution of voter preferences and party positions in Western democracies through

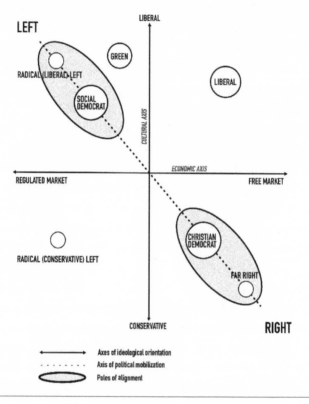

FIGURE 3.1 Ideological landscape in the twentieth century.

Source: Adjusted and adapted from Azmanova 2010, 394.

most of the twentieth century followed a left–right axis, running between the top left (socialist-liberal) and bottom right (capitalist-conservative) sectors of the ideological map (see figure 3.1).[16]

Here, a peculiarity of the twentieth-century political landscape comes to light: ideological preferences combining economic and cultural liberalism were marginal. This was a result of the policy consensus between the two centrist political families on curbing the free market via state-managed redistributive policies, a consensus enacted within the post-WWII welfare state. The agreement between conservatism and social democracy on constraining market forces has been stronger in Europe than in the United States. European conservatism, in contrast to its American counterpart, has preserved the idea of the social vocation of central authority as part of its aristocratic heritage, while U.S. political conservatism, having its pedigree in Protestantism, has always shunned institutionalized authority. Notwithstanding these differences, in both Europe and the United States a policy consensus emerged at the beginning of the twentieth century for curbing the free market, one that was institutionalized after World War II in policies designed to subject the liberal ethos of capitalism to the growth-and-redistribution domestic policy logic of Keynesianism.

The crisis of the welfare state in the 1970s fostered a novel transideological consensus on the need to free the market from political intervention. This position was embodied in the neoliberal stance of conservative parties and also in the Third Way formula many center-left parties endorsed in moving to the right on economic policy. At the same time, the center-right moved to the left on cultural issues, gradually endorsing the progressive politics of gender equality and cultural diversity that the liberal Left had initiated in the 1970s. This is truer for the European context than for the United States, where the culture wars on abortion, gun laws, homosexual rights, and the public-school history and science curricula sharpened the liberal-conservative polarization throughout the 1990s, even as a considerable part of the Republican political leadership endorsed the civil rights agenda. The familiar map of electoral politics began to shift (see figure 3.2).

Three sociocultural dynamics drove the erosion of the left–right divide and the capital–labor conflict it had expressed. First,

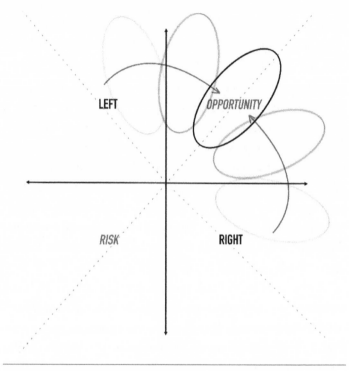

FIGURE 3.2 A shift in the poles of political alignment.

the well-documented expansion of the middle class during the three decades after World War II made the class conflict considerably less politically salient. Second, the proliferation of forms of ownership and professional tenure in the late twentieth century blurred class divisions; by investing their savings in publicly listed companies, many workers became part-owners of the means of production. Third, the management class grew in numbers, while its employment conditions equalized with those of white-collar workers. This created a large social middle—what Robert Corfe (2010) has described as the "middle-middle 90%+ majority." This made politically irrelevant whatever remained of the capital–labor divide. The process of blurring the typical divisions concerning economic class was paralleled by another one—the growing saliency of the noneconomic agenda of "postmaterial" values and risks and the shift that ensued from a class-based to a value-based system of political preferences.[17]

As a result of the post-WWII socialist–conservative policy consensus on "welfare capitalism," by the end of the 1970s it seemed that the only stable core element of the left–right contrast was between "the powers that be" and "the weak," with *left* and *right* becoming equivalent to *down* and *up* in the hierarchical distribution of political power (Laponce 1981). Ideological cross-class voting (e.g., workers voting for center-right parties) and the rise of "catch-all" parties in the late twentieth century all but erased the left–right electoral divide, without replacing it with a new overarching paradigm (McKnight 2005; Mair 2007a, 2007b; Perrineau 2002).[18] The neoliberal consensus between the center-left and the center-right of the late twentieth century replaced the post-WWII welfare state, but this shift did not reverse the waning of the left–right divide. Technocratic policy-making by governments dispensed of partisan politics, even as the content of the policy consensus altered sharply from curbing the market to freeing it. The clustering of policy positions in the center weakened the political relevancy of the left–right ideological conflicts, although the labels remained present in the language of electoral mobilization.

The space of electoral competition altered accordingly. At the very end of the twentieth century, as disagreements about economic policy almost disappeared, the main distribution of policy preferences pivoted further, aligning almost completely with the vertical axis opposing liberal to conservative/authoritarian sociocultural positions, that is, in a north–south orientation (Kitschelt 2004). The predominance of the cultural divides over the economic ones in shaping the main political families in that period was equally true for Europe and the United States. The center-left and center-right in Europe came to endorse the "free market" as a matter of political common sense, while the "culture wars" over religion, traditional gender role models, and (in the United States) gun control dominated politics.

The demise of the left–right conflict has been both lamented and celebrated. Some scholars have welcomed it, calling the party-political system that embodies it a hindrance to progressive politics in the twenty-first century (Corfe 2010). Anthony Giddens (1994) pronounced the old ideological battles obsolete in the context of postindustrial societies, advancing the formula of a Third Way that was meant to transcend "the tired dichotomy." In others' judgment, this tendency is perilous for the public welfare as centrist parties who claim to stand beyond the ideological battles are liable to be opportunistic and to deprive politics of its moral and ideational dimensions (Bobbio 1996). Moreover, the conservative–socialist cohabitation in "grand coalitions" and the style of technocratic consensus politics it generated, more than the alleged unsustainability of its economic and social policies, is what eroded the welfare state as a form of relationship between citizens and governments (Azmanova 2004, 278–79; Mouffe 2005, 29, 69–72). By the end of the twentieth century, the left–right divide that had structured politics for two centuries was not only erased, it was not being replaced by a new overarching paradigm of ideological orientation and electoral mobilization (Mair 2007). On the debris of the old ideological battles, expert rule rose to reign.

Yet, at the turn of the new century, such a new paradigm began to take shape. Unconventional parties mushroomed in many European countries—ATTAC in France, the White March movement in Belgium, the Pim Fortijn List in the Netherlands, the Margherita alliance in Italy, and the Bloco de Esquerda in Portugal—suggesting both the incapacity of expert politics to respond to public concerns and the inability of the old left–right political identifications to align comfortably with new public demands. The rise of new parties is all the more significant because it goes against the trend of small parties' terminal decline in increasingly bipolarized political systems.

In partisan terms, many of these new parties seemed to be expressing an incongruous set of convictions combining cultural liberalism with anti-Muslim sentiment, endorsement of free markets domestically, opposition to global trade, and appeals for a social safety net. Thus, Donald Trump's policy platform launched in the run-up to the presidential elections of 2016 was riddled with contradictions. He called for mass deportations of immigrants but opposed cuts to Medicare and Social Security, vowed to expand the military but criticized free trade. Such policy positions cannot be easily located on the familiar map of electoral politics structured by a left–right divide.

At the same time, electoral support for economic liberalism surged. Let us recall that parties for whom economic liberalism is a cornerstone of political identity (e.g., the Freie Demokratische Partei in Germany—the "Liberals" in figure 3.1) had stood at the margins of the left–right electoral alignment. This situation changed only with the sudden rise of electoral support for liberal parties in Europe in the first decade of the twenty-first century.[19]

The rise of "unorthodox" parties calling for both cultural and social protection, on the one hand, and, on the other, the increased electoral demand for a combination of economic and cultural liberalism seem to be shifting the main axis of public demand toward the previously sparsely populated top right and bottom left quadrants of the ideological map—that is, at odds with the traditional left–right divide. However, this is not a simple reconfiguration of political preferences; rather, it is a durable alteration of the ideological geography of Western democracies: its ideational boundaries, spaces of ideological identification, and fault lines of political conflict and cooperation. (This emergent overarching paradigm of political meaning-making and political contestation is, in turn, triggered by novel dynamics at work in the political economy of capitalist democracies. This will be explored in chapters 4 and 5.)

THE IDEOLOGICAL LANDSCAPE OF THE TWENTY-FIRST CENTURY

Toward the close of the twentieth century, a new axial principle of social stratification (distribution of life-chances) emerged in Western societies, one related to the social impact of the exposure to globalization. The new economy of open borders and technological upheaval engendered both hazards and advantages. Most importantly, losses and gains came to be unevenly distributed, incurring a complex stratification, an issue addressed in detail in the next chapter as part of the review of the transformation of democratic capitalism. For now, I will stop at the observation that the distribution of opportunities and hazards created winners and losers according to the experienced or anticipated social effect of the combination between open borders and advanced technologies.

Studies on the "losers" and "winners" from globalization are abundant. These groups are often cast in terms of the growing income gap between low-skilled and highly skilled workers (Geishecker and Görg 2007; Kapstein 2000). The saliency of globalization for political mobilization has been attributed directly to the former's material impact (Kriesi et al. 2006), but I prefer to see it in terms of attitudes to the *anticipated* distribution of globalization's opportunities and hazards (Azmanova 2004). Note, for instance, that the typical voters for the new far-right populist formations are not the unemployed, but male blue-collar workers, most employed in manufacturing, who feel threatened by the prospects of companies relocating production abroad or automating. In contrast to manufacturing, the low-tech service industry (e.g., the care and cleaning sectors) is not exposed to globalization; low-skilled workers in such employment continue to vote for the Left.

As a result, new *politically significant* divisions began emerging that guide ideological orientation and political conflict in contemporary liberal democracies. A new alliance of social forces is being formed around a "risk" (or "fear") pole of political mobilization, where parts of capital and labor align behind policies of economic patriotism, a combination of domestic market liberalization and a closed (protected) economy, as well as cultural sovereigntism, typically voiced in anti-immigrant rhetoric. On the other side of the spectrum, parties and their supporters are mobilizing who experience globalization as an advantage in terms of wealth creation and more flexible and versatile lifestyles, as well as those celebrating the promise of new technologies to mitigate climate change. The emerging new societal alliances are replacing the old left–right axis of ideological orientation with an opportunity–risk divide, shaped by attitudes to the experienced or anticipated social effect of globalization (figure 3.3).

This is not just a novel configuration of public preferences within the old map of ideological orientation. The new economy has altered the thematic framework of political interaction—what I described in chapter 2 as a "framework of political reference" (shared notions of what counts as a politically significant

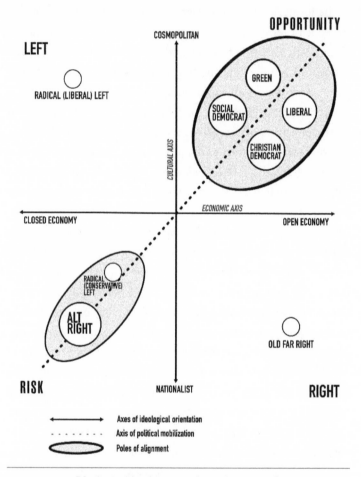

FIGURE 3.3 Ideological landscape in the early twenty-first century.

Source: Adjusted and adapted from Azmanova 2010, 400.

social issue), within which public debates about justice are artic-ulated. As notions of political saliency have altered, so has the content of the cultural and economic axes of the ideological map. Let us trace these changes, as reflected in the changed labeling of the ideological axes between figures 3.1 and 3.3.

The crisis of the welfare state in the 1970s had fostered a trans-ideological consensus on economic policy in favor of free markets. The agenda of political debate thus moved away from the dichotomy of free enterprise versus state intervention. The policy rhetoric of the welfare state had centered on economic growth, market regulation, and social transfer systems. It came to be recast around the cultural, political, and economic challenges of globalization. I discussed earlier the emergence of a new (order and security) public agenda centered on concerns with material (economic and physical) risk linked to insecurity of income and lack of physical safety. This new framework of reference structured around the opportunities and hazards of globalization has radically altered the content of the economic and cultural axes of political orientation.

The economic axis no longer denotes attitudes to state intervention in the economy (between free and regulated markets). The neoliberal consensus ended the salience of this issue altogether as Left parties shifted to the right on economic policy. Notably, not only the center left has been coopted to endorse the free market as engine of prosperity. (In the words of Nancy Pelosi, leader of the Democrats in the U.S. House of Representatives, "We're capitalist and that's just the way it is."[20]) So have been formations that identify themselves as radical Left, urging the promotion of "protected national economy organized along capitalist lines" (Harman 2007).[21] The *free-versus-regulated market* policy contention of the late twentieth century has been recast into one spanning *market openness versus closed domestic markets*. The former dichotomy concerns domestic economic policy, the latter foreign trade.[22]

The content of the cultural axis of political contestation has also altered. The progressive agenda of civil rights, identity recognition, and ecological concerns came to be accepted by center-right parties in Europe as well as by the moderate wing of the Republican Party in the United States, thereby forging what Nancy Fraser has called "progressive neoliberalism" (Fraser 2017a, 2017b). The mainstreaming of "progressive politics," together with the rise of new public concerns about political mismanagement and physical risks, has given rise to a new frame of reference spelling out issues for disagreement along the cultural axis of ideological battles. Attitudes to immigration became a key element in this new framework. Consequently, the liberal-versus-traditionalist cultural divide has been replaced by a *cosmopolitanism–versus–nationalism* dichotomy, fostered by contrasting judgments on the permeability of national borders in the context of globalization and the capacity of societies to cope with that change.

The new ideological geography of liberal democracies has a significant peculiarity: the types of alliances the new economic and cultural vectors encourage. The opportunity–risk divide cuts across capital and labor, dividing the old ideological families of the Left and the Right. A powerful alliance of social forces has been forming around the "opportunity pole"—the urban liberal upper middle class (the typical voter for environmental and socialist parties), as well as those sourcing their livelihoods from financial capital and the transnational corporations reaping the benefits of globalization (who typically support center-right parties). On the other side are poorly skilled, poorly educated workers trapped in the vanishing jobs of the old economy, as well as those well-educated young adults who have become aware that the political economy of our times no longer produces jobs, even in conditions of growth (e.g., the "hipster right"). This makes for strange bedfellows, indeed. As every policy idea is only as strong as the alliance of forces behind it, this reconfiguration of alliances is likely to have consequences far more dramatic than the electoral turbulences of 2016 and 2017.

While old and new parties have been trying to adjust to the new public demands, they have also shaped them by offering a language within which the fears of globalization have been politicized (i.e., shaped into policy issues). In this regard, the impotency of the Left and the virility of the Far Right have been momentous. The metamorphosis of the ideological map of liberal democracies has split the Left, which, throughout the twentieth century, had been the social force behind both the multiculturalism agenda domestically and the global social justice agenda internationally. As the (relative) impoverishment of the middle classes in Western societies brings the "social question" again to center stage, for the first time national social justice agendas are sharply pitted against transnational and transcultural solidarity. Globalization has placed the two in a zero-sum game. The cosmopolitan concerns, typical of the new Left, are now clashing with the growth- and redistribution-based social justice agenda of the old Left. This is among the key reasons for the Left's inability to respond to the novel concerns of its traditional constituency (the vanishing, yet anxious industrial working class). As it remained silent on these issues while the new order-and-security public agenda of social concerns was taking shape, the Right captured the vote of the Risk pole, supplying it with the easily available language of national sovereignty and democratic self-determination.

The adjustment between public demand and political supply around the opportunity–risk divide has been completed in the United States and France in the latest rounds of presidential elections, which pitted candidates mobilizing the risk pole (respectively, Donald Trump and Marine Le Pen) against candidates espousing economic and cultural liberalism (respectively, Hillary Clinton and Emmanuel Macron). The ideological positions of these four political figures cannot be easily located on the habitual ideological map of the twentieth century, but very easily situated at the "opportunity" and "risk" poles of the twenty-first century's map.

Thus, what liberal cultural elites have derided as despicable populism (the right-wing variety, on account of its xenophobia), or as naïve populism (the left-wing variety, because of its unrealistic demands for trade protectionism), is in fact a product of the fallacious misarticulation of otherwise valid public concerns about disappearing sources of livelihood. Moreover, the fact that these new unorthodox political formations are expressing reasonable and lasting concerns and policy preferences from the bottom left quadrant of the new ideological map of liberal democracies means that we should stop using the lazy and misleading label "populism." Progressive forces might still find the language and the policies to give a valiant response to the anxious publics. This book is an attempt to offer such an exit from the current impasse.

What is most disconcerting about the new ideological geography of the West is that it leaves no space for utopia—for an overarching project spelling out available opportunities for a better future *for all*. Ever since their inception in the late eighteenth century, the left–right distinctions denoted such projects. Thus, conservatism and liberalism—the two ideological traditions that the French Revolution engendered—articulated alternative paths for societal progress. By the late nineteenth century, this dichotomy was replaced by socialism to the left, liberalism in the middle, and conservatism to the right, but the logic of ideological conflict remained intact. This conflict was about the direction and means for society's development. Instead, the "opportunity" and "risk" poles of the contemporary ideological geography do not demarcate the ideological territories of groups with competing projects about society's development. The ideological battle is not about the shape of a common future, but about the allocation of the gains and losses the new economy generates. Political rivalries have turned into animosities. Former opponents are now enemies. The logic of rival utopias has been replaced by that of civil war.

With an enviable historical intuition, French high-school students in the spring of 2017 rejected these perilous ideological dynamics with the slogan "Neither Le Pen nor Macron; neither the Patriot nor the Boss—we deserve better than that!" They made it clear that replacing the neoliberal technocratic consensus with the newly emerging choice between a xenophobic populism and business-driven politics is unacceptable.[23]

By all evidence, the emancipatory project of our times not only lacks the luxury of a helpful crisis of capitalism, but cannot use the crutches of an inspiring utopia. We will return to the search for ways to unblock the "crisis of crisis" in the direction of radical transformation in chapter 7. The next task at hand is to scrutinize the socioeconomic dynamics of contemporary capitalism (chapters 4–6) in order to disclose what the changed logic of political mobilization has to do with the altered nature of the political economy of democratic capitalism. This will allow us to discern an overarching grievance behind the various experiences of injustice and the seemingly incompatible appeals to justice. This will suggest a way of transforming the logic of civil war into a logic of justice for all.

4

THE LIFE AND TIMES OF
DEMOCRATIC CAPITALISM

There must be something rotten in the very core of a social system which increases its wealth without diminishing its misery and increases its crime even more rapidly.

—Karl Marx, "Population, Crime, and Pauperism" (1859)

CONSOLIDATION, NOT CRISIS:
ON THE NON-SORRY STATE OF
CONTEMPORARY CAPITALISM

Twentieth-century civilization has collapsed. It is tempting to declare this, updating to our times the opening sentence of Karl Polanyi's 1945 opus *The Great Transformation*, which traced the collapse of nineteenth-century liberal capitalism. One of the signals of the current demise of the sociopolitical order of capitalist democracies is the thorough reshaping of their ideological landscape as reviewed in the previous chapter. I noted that the left–right divide that had shaped the ideological space and steered electoral mobilization throughout the previous century no longer allows us to make sense of the way public concerns aggregate into contrasting policy alternatives. More remarkably still, the left–right divide and the capital–labor conflict it used to represent are giving way to new fault lines of ideological orientation and political competition. These are shaped by attitudes toward the social impact of the new economy of open borders and information technology. I described this new axis as stretching between an "opportunity" and a "risk" pole, eroding old alliances and bringing together strange bedfellows. The ideological landscape, thus reconfigured, leaves no room for a utopia to inspire and guide progressive policy.

This overhaul, I suggest, is part of a larger transformation of democratic capitalism into a new modality. This postneoliberal variant, which I name "precarity capitalism" for reasons that will become clear shortly, is the fourth consecutive iteration of capitalism since its consolidation in the nineteenth century into its first "liberal" form. The novel features of this variation concern four aspects of the socioeconomic order: (1) the organization of the political economy; (2) the type of power and style of rule public authority is entitled to exercise; (3) the legitimation of power within the semantics of a new social contract (legitimacy deal); and (4) the nature of social protest and political activism.

Before laying out the distinctive features of this new modality of democratic capitalism in the next chapter, let us adumbrate the three configurations of capitalism that preceded the current one.

THE "REPERTOIRE" OF
CAPITALISM AND ITS FIRST
THREE CONFIGURATIONS

Capitalism is always in flux; it "not only never is but never can be stationary," as Joseph Schumpeter observed (1943, 82).

Capitalism has found institutional form in a variety of national models that have coexisted synchronically, as recorded in the "varieties of capitalism" literature (e.g., Hall and Soskise 2001). However, the object of my analysis is the linear transformation it has undergone from its first, liberal (entrepreneurial) modality to its current state, notwithstanding national variations. As noted in chapter 2, I see these successive forms not as distinct "epochs," but rather as overlapping reconfigurations of a "repertoire"—the set of capitalism's constitutive features. In this movement, every new form of capitalism sublimates the preceding ones (see also the appendix).

I outlined the "repertoire of capitalism" as a limited set of features that mark capitalism as a structured system of social relations. This comprises its two systemic dynamics: the competitive pursuit of profit (its constitutive dynamic and operative logic) and primitive appropriation (the secondary, enabling dynamic). In turn, certain social institutions structure the relations among participants. In the historical existence of Western capitalism, three such core institutions have played a key structuring role: the private property and management of the means of production, the "free" labor contract, and the market as a primary mechanism of economic governance (that is, for the allocation of productive inputs and social surplus). Note that this function of the market is different from the one of meeting supply and demand in the satisfaction of human needs, a function that the market has played in many social formations. The repertoire of capitalism also comprises an ethos: worldviews orienting behavior and giving it the meaning of rational enterprise under individual initiative.

Capitalism draws public support from a normative matrix that hosts the implicit understanding among citizens about what

constitutes a fair distribution of life-chances. I called this society's "legitimation matrix." Since its inception, capitalism has
relied on a certain formula for gaining the endorsement of even
the losers in the game of competitive profit production. In an
idealized market society, risks and opportunities are to be correlated for every participant; the opportunity that owners of capital have for generating wealth is (purportedly) justified by the
investment risks they undertake.[1] Workers' meager opportunities for enrichment are balanced by their allegedly smaller stake
in the economic process. (In case of a bankruptcy, an owner loses
everything, the worker, just his or her wages.) Thus, as long as
inequalities result from opportunities available to all participants
to engage in the risky business of competitive profit-creation,
they are deemed acceptable.

This repertoire of capitalism's core elements emerged as early
as the seventeenth century in Europe, within varied institutional
frameworks, from those of monarchical absolutism to the free
merchant Hanseatic cities, and consolidated as a distinct socioeconomic system in the nineteenth century. The process of consolidation, as Karl Polanyi reminds us, took place within the
institutional framework of the liberal state, itself a creation of
the self-regulating market (Polanyi 1944, 3).

I also noted in chapter 2 that shifts in what is expected from
public authority—that is, what is a properly public/political
concern—evolve under the influence of what I called a "framework of political reference," a political common sense regarding
which social phenomena are seen as politically relevant (e.g., poverty, gender equality, famine in faraway places) and what signification they acquire. In decoding the recent concerns with
inequality as the main frame of protest politics, it is useful to
recall that the intellectuals who pioneered egalitarian thinking

in the United States and Europe in the revolutionary eighteenth century did so for the sake of liberty and human dignity, not for the sake of material equality as a value in itself. They believed political and social relations should be free from all forms of domination, as Simon Reid-Henry (2015) reminds us in his investigation of the political origin and political significance of inequality. The goal has been to uproot the *kind* of inequalities that threaten human dignity and freedom, the two founding principles of early American politics. In other words, equality had a place in the framework of political reference when the foundations of capitalist democracies were being set, but acquired its particular connotation within an ethos of *nondomination*.

Alexis de Tocqueville's observations on the nascent democracy in America offer a further insight into this broader ethos shaping the original legitimation matrix of capitalist democracies. When, in the early 1830s, the young French aristocrat undertook his explorations, he was above all struck by what he called "the general equality of condition among the people" (Tocqueville [1835] 1990, 1:3). What he had in mind was not material equality (for surely American society was unequal at that time), but what he praised as equality of freedom and of political worth rooted in an emphatic rejection of privilege.[2] Are our current concerns with growing material inequality perhaps a sign that the whole ethos of capitalist democracies has shifted considerably from the original rejection of social privilege to an open endorsement of the value of equal wealth? Or is the outrage in fact a confirmation of the founding value of social rather than material equality—because economic inequality is being translated into social hierarchy? Or is the language of equality expressing an entirely different concern? We will come to this discussion in the next chapters. Let us now return to clarifying the basic components of capitalism and trace its main historical configurations.

The above-articulated understanding of the basic repertoire of capitalism has implications about the compatibility between liberal democracy as a political system and capitalism as a social system. Democracy can endorse the competitive production of profit, the key operative logic of capitalism, under two conditions: that (1) risks and opportunities are correlated for every participant; and (2) the material inequalities created in this process do not engender social privilege. In other words, we accept the inequality created in the competitive pursuit of profit as long as it does not translate into social hierarchy. This is guaranteed by the institutional logistics of equal citizenship, from equality before the law to the universal electoral franchise.

Such has been the founding contract enabling the establishment of capitalism and its consolidation in the course of the nineteenth century as an overarching system of social relations. However, the material circumstances of social life change in such a way as to disrupt the correlation between opportunities and risks; views of what counts as social risks and opportunities also alter, and so do ideas of what public authority can and should do to maintain the fair distribution of life-chances as stipulated in the original legitimation matrix. Shifts in the legitimacy deal are needed in order to maintain the normative matrix from which capitalism draws its public support. Such changes have generated four consecutive configurations of democratic capitalism. To the extent that in each the legitimacy deal between public authority and citizens manages to uphold the original legitimation matrix, capitalism has maintained its viability.

Let me now trace the way the consecutive iterations of the basic repertoire of capitalism have taken place.

Liberal Capitalism

The nineteenth century liberal form of capitalism (also known as laissez-faire capitalism) established itself by the 1860s through the massive advance of the industrial economy. This was, in the words of the historian Eric Hobsbawm, "the triumph of a society which believed that economic growth rested on the competitive private enterprise, on success in buying everything in the cheapest market (including labor) and selling in the dearest" (1975, 13). This apt formulation captures liberal capitalism's institutional logicistics as well as its normative triumph in terms of a shared societal ethos that gave it the sense of normality and desirability. This social order developed within a particular political framework—that of the liberal constitutional state committed to ensuring institutionalized autonomy for the individual. This autonomy was the foundation for the freedom of economic enterprise (laissez-faire) secured via the freedom of contract vested in law. The liberation of private enterprise that powered the progress of industry demanded the removal of institutional barriers to the free movement of the factors of production, including labor. Thus, the controls of guilds over artisan production gave way to freedom to enter any trade. Remnants of feudal law constraining but also protecting labor were abolished. In England, for example, the "annual bond" of the miners was abolished and the Master and Servant Acts were changed to establish equality of treatment for breaches of contract to both parties. In the same spirit, by the late 1870s, major legal obstacles to trade unions and to the right to strike were abolished. In turn, as the freedom of contract enabled the hiring and exploitation of formally free labor, it generated economic constraints to the institutionalized autonomy of the individual, constraints that came to be known as labor commodification (that is, treating humans' productive capacity as a good to be sold and bought).

However, capitalistic interests cannot be entirely credited for the emergence of the legal system of the modern liberal state. With Max Weber, we might say that they "undoubtedly . . . helped, but by no means alone and nor even principally" ([1904–1905] 1992, 25). The form of capitalism that Weber deemed to be unique to the modern West—the rational capitalistic organization of formally free labor—is correlated to the institutional setup of liberal constitutionalism via a particular mindset he calls "Occidental rationalism," or "the ability and disposition of men to adopt certain types of practical rational conduct" (26). Worldviews valorizing and motivating rational enterprise under individual initiative are a key component of this mindset. Thus liberalism, in this first modality of capitalism, was not simply a norm governing the realm of economic action. It was rather a spiritual mindset, a Zeitgeist, and as such assumed the status of "the organizing principle of a society engaged in creating a market system" within the institutional framework of the liberal state (Polanyi 1944, 135).

The nominal separation between economics and politics was a core feature of the first legitimacy deal (that is, the idea that public authority should not privilege economic actors and in turn economic power should not influence politics). This was forged by the liberal state with the separation of powers, legal safeguards against unlawful interference with the rights of privacy and property, and other institutional paraphernalia typical of liberal politics. This provided the political setting for liberal capitalism; it became "the irrefragable condition of the existing system of society" (Polanyi 1944, 225). In this first modality of capitalism, the behavior-orienting value of individual entrepreneurial action—"hard work" with its attendant risks and rewards—molds the semantics of collective social and political existence.

Welfare Capitalism

By the end of the nineteenth century, the free market had allocated considerably more risks to wage laborers and others who had little or no opportunity to make real gains in the economy, while putting them in inhumane, life-threatening conditions. This endangered the legitimacy matrix of capitalism by violating the ground rule of correlating opportunities and risks. A severe legitimacy crisis followed, entailing the collapse of the system, as surveyed by Karl Polanyi in *The Great Transformation* (1944). What followed was a large-scale policy effort to restore the balance between opportunity and risk via building a social safety net by, for instance, introducing stable employment contracts and unemployment insurance and limiting working hours and working lives.

This transformation resulted in the reconstitution of capitalism after World War II into a new modality—what scholars in the Frankfurt School tradition have discussed as "advanced," or "late" capitalism, and Scott Lash and John Urry (1987) named "organized capitalism." It developed within the institutional format of the welfare state committed to the democratization of prosperity. This is why I prefer to refer to it as "welfare capitalism." The New Deal in the United States and the welfare state in Europe were distinct forms of welfare capitalism, whose key features were state regulation of the economy, nationalization/socialization of some key economic sectors, a main economic policy objective of subordinating profitability to growth, and aiding the survival of private capital through government orders, direct subsidies, or fiscal policy.

It is relevant to recall that the catalyst for the birth of this second modality of capitalism was the broad societal movement that had already emerged at the waning of the nineteenth century against the economic dogma of the self-regulating ("free") market. This collectivist countermovement, Karl Polanyi notes, was a broad societal undertaking that "was not due to any preference for socialism or nationalism on the part of concerted interests, but exclusively to the broader range of the vital social interests affected by the expanding market mechanism" (1944, 145).[3] In other words, while entrepreneurial capital had been reaping the benefits of the free market arrangement, the social risks fell excessively to wage labor. This situation was unacceptable from the perspective of the basic legitimation matrix of democratic capitalism stipulating that opportunities and risks in the distribution of life-chances should be correlated.

As the civil and political society mobilized to restore this balance, a new framework of political reference emerged, which came to include poverty and precariousness as politically salient social phenomena. Thus, in this iteration, the scope of the legitimation matrix of capitalist democracies regarding the distribution of life-chances expanded to include the idea of social justice codified in social rights alongside the political and civil liberties and the value of economic entrepreneurship that had been political cornerstones of liberal capitalism. In turn, the legitimacy deal between citizens and public authority adjusted to include the state's duty of protecting society from the market. In the previous constellation, the market alone was meant to ensure the balance between opportunities and risks that rendered capitalism legitimate, and it was the purview of families and churches to take care of the weakest.

The political legitimacy of democratic capitalism after WWII came to rely on a notion of justice surpassing both that of political equality, which is fundamental to *democracy*, and that of individual entrepreneurship, which is fundamental to *capitalism*. To bridge economic entrepreneurship with political equality, the state was tasked with a new legitimacy-conferring function— that of redistribution of wealth for the purpose of securing the conditions for social justice. The *social* responsibility of public authority was born as a centerpiece of the new legitimacy deal: in addition to maintaining the economic machine of prosperity (the free market), the state also became responsible for addressing the consequences of the process of prosperity creation for society at large. The latter element, which we could call "socially responsible rule," can be equated with neither *accountable* rule achieved via periodic elections and checks and balances nor with *responsive* rule, policies in direct response to public demands. Rather, socially responsible rule is a matter of public authority's willingness to take into consideration the social impact of its policies (Azmanova 2013b).

A variety of institutional models gave shape to the social partnership among organized capital, organized labor, and a democratic state that marked welfare capitalism. This is captured along the "varieties of capitalism" and "varieties of welfare regimes" taxonomies, which I will refrain from reviewing here.[4] Instead, I will refer generally to "welfare capitalism" as the modality that persisted from WWII through the 1970s. Welfare capitalism was characterized by an organized and institutionalized political collectivism that existed on two levels: within the realm of political economy as corporatism (the power of organized economic interests),[5] and within the realm of political competition as mass, class-based parties competing along a left–right axis of ideological orientation and forming the large political families of socialism and conservatism. Both in the sphere of the economy and party politics, competition among ideas and products was tamed by collective bargaining. Political intervention into the operation of markets was a key feature of the political economy of welfare capitalism. It took two forms: (1) state *regulation* of the interactions among economic actors, itself based on corporatist negotiations, and (2) some degree of *public ownership* (socialization) of the economy. Giant oligopolies towered over the national economies, their executives acting as "corporate statesmen," sometimes even sacrificing profits for the sake of a perceived social good (Reich 2007). Business leaders had no choice but to be constrained by considerations of the common good because their businesses were embedded within and therefore dependent on territorially bounded societies.

This second modality has been both celebrated as a triumph of democracy over capitalism and vilified as the triumph of corporate interests over society. This captures its dialectical nature, for it is indeed both, having established a capital–labor alliance in support of capitalism around the value of national economic growth and the democratization of prosperity through mass consumerism. Welfare capitalism left as its progressive heritage a lasting conception of social rights, together with the institutional toolset for ensuring them. But it gave this conception of social justice a heavily consumerist underpinning that incurred severe environmental costs.

In the analyses developed by Frankfurt School authors such as Theodor Adorno, Herbert Marcuse, and Jürgen Habermas, the shift from liberal to state-managed welfare capitalism entailed a rationalization of capital mediated by the state, a process in which the technical rationality of economic and administrative efficiency starts to pervade all aspects of human action. The politicization of economic production, together with the development of the culture industry, destroys the spaces of individual autonomy available under liberal capitalism. Organized interests both on the side of workers and on the side of employers consolidated the power of labor-market insiders at the expense of society at large (Habermas 1973) and of ethnic minorities and women, who were often denied access to the labor market. Moreover, the technocratic consensus on state-managed capitalism had a nefarious effect on politics because it diminished ideological competition.

Numerous factors combined in bringing welfare capitalism to its demise in the 1970s.[6] Among the most popular explanations is the perception, at least in influential policy circles, that the constraints the state had put on capital under the pressures of organized labor had hampered capitalism as an engine of prosperity. Costly social insurance and cumbersome regulation of product and labor markets had allegedly limited capital's opportunities for profit-making and reduced the incentives for risk-taking on which it purportedly thrives. The matrix was endangered. Democratic capitalism had to be reinvented yet again.

Neoliberal Capitalism

After the 1970s, welfare capitalism came under policy pressures for freeing the economy from state intervention. The result was what came to be known as neoliberal capitalism.[7] British prime minister Margaret Thatcher officially inaugurated neoliberalism in the 1980s with what she called the "TINA" policy dictum: There Is No Alternative to the combination of free markets and open economies.[8] This doctrine secured the transideological policy consensus between the center-left and center-right party leaderships around the Third Way policy formula, which technocratic elites allegedly free of ideological bias enacted in the last two decades of the twentieth century. The rise of technocracy had already taken place with the growth of the bureaucratic machinery under welfare capitalism. The novel element was that, under the guise of "meritocracy," it was invested with the newly redeemed ethos of individualism that credits achievement through personal merit and in conditions of fair competition.

The transition to neoliberal capitalism was facilitated by the convergence between criticism of welfare capitalism from the political Left and the political Right. On the left, the target of discontent was the oppressive bureaucratization of the economy and political life, as well as the privileges accruing to labor-market insiders. On the right, it was the power of organized labor to raise remuneration, which allegedly hampered productivity. On the thinning legitimacy of welfare capitalism, a new consensus was forged between the political families of the center left and the center right: the former accepted free market capitalism, the latter endorsed the New Left agenda of progressive politics centered on identity recognition. Thus, the hegemony of "progressive neoliberalism" was secured, as discussed in the previous chapter.

This ideological consensus among political elites rested on a deeper foundation: the capital–labor alliance in support of national economic growth that had been forged under welfare capitalism. This was the enabling mechanism that secured a transideological policy consensus for rebooting the engine of capitalism by deploying three sets of policies: (1) privatization of companies and sectors of the economy that had been previously in public hands; (2) deregulation of labor and product markets, including financial services; and (3) opening of national economies for free trade.

Combined, these policy reforms and the development of information technologies in the late twentieth century created what Robert Reich has called "supercapitalism." Intensified competition broke down the large corporations that had dominated the political economy of welfare capitalism, with firms becoming smaller, far more competitive, global, and innovative, but also less socially responsible as they catered exclusively to the interests of consumers and shareholders (Reich 2007).

Thus, although preserving some institutional variation and altogether resisting a full convergence, the national models of welfare capitalism were subjected to common pressures of neoliberal transformation. These transformative dynamics have been broadly described as "disorganization" of capitalism: a breakdown of the mechanisms that had previously ensured, through mediation, a dynamic balance between social power and political authority (Offe 1985, 6). This is often cast in terms of liberalization and deregulation of the economy for the sake of enhancing market efficiency, "a trend in the political economy away from centralized authoritative coordination and control, towards dispersed competition, individual instead of collective action, and spontaneous, market-like aggregation of preferences and decisions" (Streeck 2009, 149). As a result of this "capitalist perestroika," the hierarchical Fordist work structure that had emerged in the early twentieth century and had been predominant in the period of welfare capitalism eventually dissolved into a new flexible, network-based form of organization (Castells 1996; Boltanski and Chiapello 1999).

Tellingly, even trade-union activity changed its nature as labor-market liberalization, accepted under the threat of losing jobs, became a central object of agreement (Streeck 1984; Rhodes 2001). The idea of social justice that had become a central element in the legitimation matrix of democratic capitalism under state-managed welfare capitalism underwent a significant change under neoliberalism. Access to the labor market (obtaining and keeping a job) became a central value. Thus, notions of social justice have shifted from the original concerns with decent working conditions and standards of living secured through a solid and stable salary toward preoccupations with one's employability and capacity to retain a job—a move from social "security" to "resilience."

The legitimation matrix in this third variety of the capitalist repertoire is shaped by a new ethos. This "new spirit of capitalism" (Boltanski and Chiapello 1999) is not so much the proud endorsement of hard work that had anchored the liberal modality, as a free spirit that celebrates self-fulfillment through initiative and autonomy, thereby co-opting the libertarian currents of the late 1960s for the purposes of endless capital accumulation. "Work smart, not hard" was the motto of this capitalism-with-sex-appeal.

The core legitimating principle of correlating opportunities and risks that had emerged under liberal capitalism remained valid under neoliberal capitalism. While under welfare capitalism the concept of risk was enlarged to take into consideration a wider range of disadvantages (social rights were perceived in the broader terms of a standard of living rather than in terms of minimal safeguards against poverty), the neoliberal notion of risk came to focus on exposure to global markets. Indicative of this is the strong corollary that has been established since the 1980s between risk management and the compensation demands of chief executives in investment banks. This is in perfect alignment with the logic of coupling risk and reward, but adapted to the neoliberal condition. The spectacular remuneration to owners and managers of financial capital has been justified, so the narrative goes, by the risks these captains of industry take in the open, unruly seas of international finance, which itself is celebrated as the wellspring of global capitalism. The deficiency of both social protest and intellectual critique targeting the political economy of neoliberal capitalism in the "roaring 1990s" is telling of the broad societal endorsement of this model. Not surprisingly, the left–right divide on economic policy vanished toward the end of the century. Not only did the main ideological families embrace free and open markets, but social activism and intellectual critique lost interest in the economy altogether. Critical theory, instead, got busy with deliberative democracy.

Enter precarity capitalism.

5

PRECARITY CAPITALISM

Despotism is unjust to everybody, including the despot, who was probably made for better things.

—Oscar Wilde, *The Soul of Man Under Socialism* (1891)

W elcome to the new dark ages," opens Peter Fleming's *The Death of Homo Economicus* (2017). "If Neoliberalism is probably dead, then what do we have in its place?" (1, 22). In earlier works, I noted the emergence of a postneoliberal model of capitalism in the early twenty-first century, which I will now proceed to examine in fuller detail, tracing both the processes that led to the eclipsing of the neoliberal form and the substantive features of the new model.[1]

An early word of clarification: I have chosen to label the current form "precarity capitalism" because, as I will discuss at length in the next chapter, economic and social insecurity has become a core feature of our societies. While in the previous models the correlation between risks and opportunities created a relative stability, the active offloading of social risk to society, as we shall see, has created a condition of generalized precarity from which the labor-market insiders—those who are skilled and have well-paying jobs—are not sheltered. Precarity is the social question of the twenty-first century.

Neoliberal capitalism fathered precarity capitalism some time at the close of the previous century. The neoliberal policy package of free (nonregulated) economies and open markets (national economies open for free trade) intensified globalization. It was this combination between a return to the laissez-faire formula in national economies and opening those economies to global competition that decided the nature of global capitalism at that time, as the rulebook of the World Trade Organization—the institutional engine of globalization—forced the economic philosophy of privatization and deregulation across the world. In turn, the social and political effects of the neoliberal globalization triggered the recasting of the parameters of democratic capitalism into a new, sequentially fourth modality. This alteration took place well before the 2007–2008 economic meltdown.

In the times of neoliberalism, national political leaders saw the opening of domestic markets as a means for pursuing the growth agenda they had inherited from welfare capitalism. However, the global market transformed rapidly from an entity composed of interlinked national economies integrated through trade agreements into transnational production networks. The liberalization of foreign direct investment was the main driver of this transformation. The financial contribution of these production networks to particular national economies became unclear and uncertain. In the new circumstances of closely integrated markets, global production chains, and intensified competition, maintaining the competitiveness of national economies became a top policy concern. Thus, at the beginning of our century, national competitiveness in the global economy became an intensely salient element in the framework of political relevance of Western democracies. Global competitiveness replaced both growth (the priority of welfare capitalism) and maintaining competition within unencumbered domestic markets (a priority under neoliberal capitalism). This shift first became conspicuous in the Lisbon Strategy, the EU policy agenda that was adopted by the European Council in 2000; subsequent revisions have made the emphasis on global competitiveness more acute.[2] The objective of global competitiveness has generated a transideological policy consensus that is embraced by capital and labor and enforced by public authority at the state level as well as in supranational bodies such as the European Union. Governments across the political spectrum rushed to implement so-called structural adjustment reforms as part of national strategies for international competitiveness (Rueda 2006).

The shift from *competition* to *competitiveness* as a policy priority implies a significant change in state–market and state–society relations. Within the paradigm of competition as a constitutive attribute of the free market, the role of public authority is to ensure a level playing field among economic agents, not only by active liberalization and deregulation of the economy, but also via legal action through antitrust law against the creation of monopolies. This has been the avowed formula of neoliberal capitalism. We might recall that increased competitive pressures in the late twentieth century had incurred the breakdown of the great oligopolies and the proliferation of economic actors.

However, with the new political commitment of increasing the competitiveness of national economies in the global market, the state began taking on the duty to aid specific economic actors—those who are best positioned to perform well in the global competition for profit. Although it has been a long-established practice for the private sector to feed off the state's initial investment in product development and innovation (Schumpeter 1943; Reich 2007; Mazzucato 2013), a peculiarity of the new form of capitalism is that public authority handpicks the companies on which to bestow this privilege. This results in the deliberate creation by the state of market monopolies. This, however, dramatically alters the distribution between opportunities and risks, as opportunities for wealth creation are actively *aggregated* to those economic actors who already have an advantage in the globally integrated markets, while risks are offloaded to the weakest players.

The inception of precarity capitalism was caused by extreme liberalization of the economy via privatization and deregulation, which took place in the neoliberal 1980s and 1990s. In that period, even sectors of the economy that in principle cannot be properly exposed to competition (energy infrastructure, rail transportation, broadband) were privatized and deregulated, thus giving their owners and managers the privileged status of rentiers. Because of low exposure to competition, this status is marked by reduced risk and high earnings. State policy has subsequently consolidated this stratified reordering of the market between a few large winners and numerous small losers, which seems to run against the tenets of liberal and neoliberal capitalism: in fact, it should endanger the foundational legitimacy matrix of capitalism, with its ground rule that opportunities and risks should be correlated. Let us scrutinize this development to understand why no legitimation crisis of capitalism has been triggered.

To a considerable extent, the unusual stratification of economic positions is the doing of that godchild of neoliberal capitalism, globalization. Globalization's transformative effect on our societies runs along two trajectories: open markets and information technology, which I have discussed as, respectively, its "quantitative" and "qualitative" dimensions (Azmanova 2011a). These channel the distribution of life-chances (social opportunities and risks) in the global economy. Indeed, individuals and firms equipped to profit from the new economy of open borders and technological innovation have seen their fortunes and social status rise.[3] To reap the benefits of economies of scale, leading firms embarked on mergers and acquisitions, creating giant corporations.[4] This rapidly reversed the tide of breaking down the great oligopolies that had been a feature of neoliberal capitalism.

Significantly, the distribution of life-chances in this context cuts across capital and labor. Both groups engaged in the old economy have become more exposed to risk resulting from higher exposure to competition, reliance on cheap labor (the effect of trade liberalization), or the incapacity to link factors of production to information technology (IT). Companies that have found ways of using IT's particular advantage—inexpensive equipment that reduces reliance on human labor while increasing the scope and speed of market access—have experienced a significant increase in the rates of return on their investment.[5]

Risks and opportunities have become decoupled and their distribution strongly stratified in the current configuration of state–market relations. This was initiated in the late twentieth century as a consequence of the withdrawal of the state from the market. It enabled the formation of monopolies by stealth due to lack of policy action beyond deregulation. By the early twenty-first century, ruling elites came to pursue this policy road via deliberate aid to companies that could help enhance national competitiveness. Special tax regimes, funding the research and development needs of private companies, and other redistributive measures amounted to systematic transfers from society to the strongest economic players. In this sense, we can speak of institutionalized aggregation of opportunities and risks. The publicly funded bank bailout in Europe and the United States was only the most advertised example of this phenomenon, best illustrated by the proliferation of so-called national champions, companies whose competitiveness in the global economy is nurtured by state policy, as demonstrated by the increased volume of "state aid" litigation at the European Commission since the turn of the century.[6] The special support states provided to specific companies during the economic crisis, especially in the automotive industry, is another instance of official policy privileging select economic actors at the expense of others. So, at this writing, is the U.S. administration's penchant for negotiating with specific companies to repatriate production from abroad, with the promise of specific perks. Similar is the logic behind the European Commission's June 2017 proposal to give European arms companies €1.5 billion per year to help develop new military technologies: while the ownership of the products resulting from this public investment would remain with the private companies, the stated objective is to support the competitiveness of the European military industry within the global market.[7]

One of the first instances of open political endorsement of "national champions" was the politically managed deal arranging the access of mobile-technology company Qualcomm to the Chinese market. It is worth looking at the way the case evolved in order to highlight the contrast with the preceding neoliberal modality, when access to the globally integrated economy was done mainly through removing obstacles to competition. In the mid-1990s, mobile phone adoption was taking off globally, with the U.S. and EU standards for wireless technology (the Code Division Multiple Access, or CDMA, and the Global System for Mobile Communications, or GSM, respectively) competing for global dominance. The Clinton administration negotiated with the Chinese government to let one U.S. company—Qualcomm—operate on the Chinese market, which resulted in the obliteration of the European standard (Barboza 2017).

Although public authority's support for businesses through industrial policy has been a well-established practice since the 1930s, the novelty is the political protection given to hand-picked companies in the hope of gaining national advantage in the world economy. The much-reprimanded penchant of U.S. president Donald Trump to negotiate deals with and for specific companies—for example, excluding Apple's iPhone, produced in China, from the 2019 tariffs he imposed on other Chinese imports—is in fact inscribed within a policy logic already established at the close of the twentieth century.

Importantly, these practices of public authority's actively and openly privileging select companies preceded the economic crisis by at least a decade. The complicity between large business and the state had already been a feature of the second modality of capitalism, one that was institutionally solidified, if not enabled, in the United States through campaign finance rules. However, while in the previous models the complicity between corporations and public authority was a matter of the penetration of corporate interests into the decisional mechanisms of the state more or less by stealth, it is currently public authority that actively and proudly pursues this as a matter of economic policy, with full public endorsement. This is done with the conviction that this is the only way to satisfy the imperative for remaining competitive in the global economy—a new and very powerful element in the legitimation deal between citizens and public authority.

The transformation of the global economy into an oligopoly (a state of limited competition, in which a market is shared by a small number of companies) has been presented as the death of competition, and even the corruption of capitalism (Standing 2016; Tepper and Hearn 2018). However, market dominance is the telos and the implied goal of competition; it is therefore a confirmation of competition as a constitutive dynamic of capitalism. The dominating companies could at any point be unseated, as long as the *principle* of competitive pursuit of profit remains intact.

Financial capital has been one of the biggest winners in the new redistribution of advantage to the already-advantaged. The "too big to fail" policy rationale has been widely discussed and I will not dwell on it. I prefer to stress the commodification of investment risk as a peculiar mechanism for this institutionalized aggregation of opportunity to financial capital. This consists of packaging leveraged financial products and selling them as profit-creating goods, a situation in which the risk contained in the package is the primary entity generating profit. From an undesirable side effect, risk thus becomes a profit-generating entity itself, one explicitly produced for market exchange—i.e., a commodity. The commodification of risk is most apparent in the case of credit default swaps (CDS).[8] In contrast to standard insurance, which we take on a life, house, or other property we own, CDS allows us to insure what we do not own—namely the risk of someone else's defaulting on a loan. Thus, contemporary capitalism has added a new specimen to the original arsenal of *fictitious* commodities (land, labor, and money). Risk is a fictitious commodity in the sense that it cannot be produced exclusively for market exchange; it remains deeply rooted in the fabric of social relations, which endow it with identification as a profit-generating entity.[9]

The commodification of financial risk has been one of the primary causes of the economic crisis of 2007–2008. When lenders withdrew their trust in the value of the risk accumulated by financial institutions and that risk exploded, public authorities, in most cases, intervened to socialize the risk via publicly funded bank bailouts. This amounted to dumping investment risk on society while opportunities for returns on investment remained in the hands of bank managers and shareholders. The recapitalization of financial institutions with public money while the ownership of these institutions remained in private hands violated capitalism's ground rule of correlating risks and opportunities. The legitimation matrix of capitalism was endangered again.

The combination of the state's sponsoring select businesses and not requiring them to have accountability (i.e., active support without sanctions) alters the behavior of the big players, who embark on aggressive opportunism "characterized by the logic of extraction rather than production" (Fleming 2017, 22). In this sense, the current form of capitalism is marked by what Peter Fleming describes as "wreckage economics," which is about "capture, not innovation, production or even growth" (40–86, 51).

It is this aggregation of risks and their allocation to society and its weakest members that transformed the financial crisis into a social crisis as governments began to cut funds for essential social services (especially health and education) in order to restore balance to their finances. In this sense, the social crisis that marked the decade after the 2007–2008 financial meltdown was triggered by the manner in which governments reacted. It was not generated by an economic crisis, a decline in business activity and general prosperity due to, say, the outsourcing of essential production to Asia in conditions of globally integrated markets.[10]

The crisis of capitalism that beset precarity capitalism in the first decade of its existence was transformed into a curious phenomenon I called the "crisis of the crisis of capitalism"—a situation marked by making the crisis a new normal instead of solving it (see chapter 1). While dealing with the 2007–2008 financial meltdown and its immediate aftermath, governments implemented emergency crisis management measures meant to be short-term stabilization mechanisms. But over the next decade, they institutionalized these as permanent solutions instead of inaugurating policies targeting the fundamental causes of the crisis—the political economy of "precarity capitalism." Examples abound. European leaders set up a fund to compensate people who lost jobs to globalization rather than undertake a revision of the main trade agreements that generated these job losses. Politics of economic patriotism in the style of Prime Minister Gordon Brown's "British Jobs of British Workers" have been endorsed as a matter of course. Central banks have repurchased the bad debt of banks, a flagship crisis-management move. This means that even after the emergency measures come to an end and economies return to growth, the debt these banks hold will restrain public spending for a long time, perpetuating austerity—and with that, precarity—as the new normal.

The use of crisis management to prolong the problem goes beyond economic policy. Authorities in Europe and the United States are shutting out asylum-seekers rather than investing resources in their proper accommodation and integration into society. In June 2017, British prime minister Theresa May pledged to limit human rights, purportedly to fight terrorism.[11] At their September 2016 summit in Bratislava, EU heads of governments endorsed the idea of "flexible solidarity," allowing countries to choose between taking in refugees and funding border protection such as the European Border and Coast Guard Agency. Under the pressure of public opinion, the EU has come to rely on autocratic regimes (Turkey) and military dictatorships (Egypt) to push migration processing offshore in "disembarkation platforms" rather than counter the hostility to immigrants by ensuring the livelihoods of workers who feel threatened or displaced.

We are losing the security not only of our employment but also of our freedoms.

As these policy measures for coping with the crisis do not eliminate its sources, we are stuck in perpetual crisis management. The sense of being in crisis is withering away and talk of crisis is subsiding. However, we are getting used to that state of affairs that initially stirred the talk of a terminal crisis of capitalism.[12]

The social crisis did bring to light a crisis of the legitimation matrix of capitalism: the ground rule stipulating the fair distribution of risk and opportunity among market actors has been violated by the accumulation of opportunities for gains without penalty of failure to a few privileged market actors, while the risks have been directed to society. This prompted relations between state and society to be politicized afresh, as voiced by the protest call "We are the 99 percent."

SOCIALLY IRRESPONSIBLE, POLITICALLY RESPONSIVE RULE

In the transformation of state–market relations since the turn of the century, the status of public authority has altered considerably. In recent years, public authority at state, EU, and international levels is taking ever more action to enhance market efficiency for the sake of global competitiveness. It is doing this by means of redistribution from the weak to the strong, using the interventionist toolset it had acquired during welfare capitalism. This has led to a dramatic increase in social risk, for which this same public authority has ceased to assume responsibility. This has brought about a type of politics we can call "socially irresponsible rule" (Azmanova 2013b): rule that disregards the social consequences of economic policy such as growing inequality, poverty, and social precariousness, even as growth is effectively obtained.

This is particularly evident in the evolution of social policy in the European Union. EU integration has reduced the policy-making powers of member states in welfare provision, while EU institutions have increasingly undertaken action in this field (Leibfried 2010), culminating in the inauguration of the so-called European Pillar of Social Rights in 2017. However, this process also erodes the social safety net because the hierarchy of EU policy competencies as vested in its treaties subordinates social policy to economic policy.

The core commitment of the EU, at least since the Single European Act of 1987,[13] has been to ensure the "four freedoms": the free movement of goods, services, capital, and people. This commitment has been persistently interpreted in the sense of free markets, although in principle open markets are not synonymous with free ones.[14] Moreover, while the EU has *exclusive* competency in matters regarding the four freedoms, it has only *shared* competencies in matters of social policy with member states. The principle of supremacy of EU law over national law, with a focus on economic freedoms,[15] establishes a de facto subordination of social policy to economic policy. As EU economic policy is laissez-faire in nature in order to facilitate the creation of a common market, this results in a minimal form of welfare provision and a race to the bottom in social protection. It is this logic that led the European Court of Justice, via its judgments in the Viking and Laval cases in December 2017, to transform the principle of *equal pay for equal work* into *minimum pay for equal work*.[16] The measures for further economic integration deemed necessary to stabilize the euro amid the Eurozone sovereign-debt crisis of 2010–2012—i.e., the adoption of a European (financial) Stability

Mechanism,[17] a Fiscal Compact (austerity pact),[18] and a banking union—narrows further the decisional powers of national parliaments regarding public revenue and spending. It will all but wipe out social policy. Within a similar logic of prioritizing the creation of an intra-European free market, the European Charter of Social Rights aims at equalizing employment conditions across member states, not at strengthening the social safety net as its name might suggest.

The same logic operates at international level. World Trade Organization law has proven to have the strongest binding power compared to other functional international regimes such as the World Labor Organization. While the 1948 Havana Charter establishing the international trade regime also dealt with social issues, the functional specialization and institutionalization of trade within the WTO in 1995 allowed the emancipation of the global free market from society. Like the relationship between economic and social policy in the EU that is shaped by the hierarchy of EU law, this means that international economic policy committed to free markets not only subordinates social policy, but also permeates it, altering its nature. Thus, EU social policy increasingly focuses on educating and retraining workers to help them enter the labor market, but does very little to secure their rights outside of employment. The claim is that public authority no longer possesses the financial resources for a robust social safety net.

Consequently, far from the expected retreat of the state under the forces of globalization (as per the neoliberal credo), we are facing the new phenomenon of governing bodies possessing increased power and capacity to inflict social harm and decreased responsibility for the social consequences of policy action. This began with the transition, in the 1980s, to what Giandomenico Majone (1990) described as "the regulatory state": one that gives priority to the use of legal authority and regulation over other tools of stabilization and redistribution. A peculiarity of this style of regulation is that it is individual-based. However, this gradually entailed individuals' becoming not just *addressees*, but *agents* of social policy. People have become increasingly charged with responsibility for issues ranging from maintaining healthy lifestyles to protecting the environment, remaining employable, finding jobs, and securing pensions. This policy logic is being enacted in the push to force information technology companies such as Facebook and Twitter, which are providing a public space for communication, to not only provide privacy protection but also act as publishers responsible for the content on their platforms. Responsibility for the content of information as well as for whom to grant access to the public space endows these private economic actors with the power to sanction the use of public space, something only a public power should have. Much as this push for the responsibility of powerful private economic actors is celebrated as a triumph for democracy, it in fact amounts to giving power to the greatest economic powerhouses.[19]

Such absolution of the state from its social responsibility is reflected even in measures intended deliberately to enhance social protection, such as the Council of Europe's Charter on Shared Social Responsibilities, adopted in 2014 after a broad public consultation. The charter advocates shared responsibilities among various social actors on grounds that states are no longer able to fund a social safety net. Similar logic underlies UNESCO's policy shift: in its 2017–2018 Global Education Monitoring Report titled "Accountability in Education: Meeting Our Commitments," the notion of accountability, for which funds are not needed, replaces responsibility, and the latter term often features as "collective responsibility."

Among the mechanisms of neoliberal governance that are also actively used in the stage of precarity capitalism is public authority's devolution. This idea has been promoted in the name of democracy, in the style of "democratization of everyday life" advocated by self-proclaimed "progressive" forces. On the right, the call for more democracy tends to put the emphasis on society rather than on the state, and demands for more democracy relate to communities' assuming more social responsibilities rather than making the government more accountable to the people. An example is the experimentation by the Conservative government in the UK with "Big Society," in which social problems are addressed through the extension of democracy by "empowering active and responsive citizenship," particularly when addressing environmental, social, and health problems.

Though such moves are often celebrated as "more democracy," we should remember that devolution of power and responsibility does not equal local empowerment. It means that large-scale problems such as unemployment or environmental degradation are offloaded onto individuals, companies, or communities that are poorly equipped to cope with them (Brown 2015). This creates a framework in which individuals are not so much free as "forced to take charge of their own life" (Beck and Beck-Gernsheim 2002, 32). The shifting of social responsibility to individuals and communities is a common feature of neoliberal and precarity capitalism and marks an important continuity between the two. The new element under precarity capitalism is that public authority actively redistributes resources from the losers to the winners and justifies this by reference to expected increase of the national economy's global competitiveness. Thus, precarity capitalism presupposes a highly capacious state with a well-developed institutional ability to intervene in the economy and society (as inherited from the stage of welfare capitalism), but combines this with strongly decreased social responsibility.

Let us trace the shifts in the "legitimacy deal," the transformation of state–society relations since the inception of democratic capitalism in the nineteenth century. Public authority under liberal capitalism purported to ensure the autonomy of the individual in a modus we can call the "teenage state." Young (in historical terms) entrepreneurs could reap all the rewards because they were on their own taking the risks, as per the normative matrix of capitalism. However, support for the system eroded as social risks overburdened workers and society in general. The transideological consensus between European socialism and European conservatism on the need to safeguard society from vagarious market forces supplied the political grammar of the post-WWII welfare state—the "nanny state." The poorly remunerated but devoted nanny would nurture the economy, pampering both entrepreneurs and workers, and with that rekindle fate in the capacity of capitalism to deliver prosperity for all. However, as the economic engine of capitalism experienced difficulties in the 1970s and could no longer deliver the promised prosperity, an alternative formula emerged. During the third, neoliberal stage, the matrix of state–society relations was rebuilt on the seemingly empowering notion of individual self-reliance in chasing exciting opportunities, what Boltanski and Chiapello (1999) called "the new spirit of capitalism." Thus, the "nanny state" of welfare capitalism was replaced by the "stepmother state" of the neoliberal 1980s and 1990s, a state that used its authority and institutional means to enforce personal self-reliance rather than simply make room for it, as in liberal capitalism. The role of the state has been further altered in recent years to allow it to actively manage the distribution of opportunities and risks via a new type of intervention: one intended to lend support to those economic actors who are best placed to ensure the competitiveness of national economies in the global marketplace. To expand the tired family metaphor, I have called this the "rich uncle state" (Azmanova 2013a). The uncle actively supports the most gifted among the siblings for the sake of securing the family business. The bright niece has all the opportunities, at a minimum risk. The rest of the family stay in the game out of fear, which has become the main motivational resource, the "spirit" of precarity capitalism.

Well before the financial meltdown, the correlation between economic opportunity and risk and the state's duty to enforce it—which are the ground rules in the legitimation matrix of democratic capitalism—came undone. As the combination of domestic market liberalization and open-market policies intensified competition, both risks and opportunities proliferated, while their distribution became strongly uneven. Under such circumstances we can reasonably expect the legitimacy of the system to suffer some damage, as had been the case in the early twentieth century.

Indeed, the thinning legitimacy of the current social order has been most acutely expressed in protests about inequality and privilege. Inequality in wealth (and thus, difference in consumption capacity) allows amplification of the opportunities the affluent already have, while the risks accrue to those who are already weak. Thomas Piketty's findings (2014) are so disturbing not because they offer impressive statistical evidence for something we have known all along—that market societies are economically unequal, and increasingly so. The upsetting part is the disclosure of the mechanism that amplifies the opportunities for those who are already advantaged, without the penalty of exposure to considerable risk. If the rate of return on capital, as a rule, outstrips the growth rate of the economy, as Piketty makes clear, this means that people with the capacity to invest their nonconsumed wealth in the stock market, especially if their capital is large enough to allow diversification of investment risk, have additional opportunities unavailable to those who lack surplus wealth to invest. If this added opportunity comes without effort and without the corresponding penalty of risk-taking (as, say, an investment in the real economy would be), then this violates the basic principles that made capitalism palatable for democracy. The public outrage over the reckless conduct of financial capital and the privileges of the affluent is thus wholly justified; it does not stem from a frivolous envy over superior consumption capacity. It is anger with undeserved opportunities while society is being put at risk.

WANTED: A LEGITIMATION CRISIS

Social unrest against inequality and privilege has intensified, as captured in the "We are the 99 percent" slogan of the Occupy movement, which sprang up in New York in the autumn of 2011 and spread to more than nine hundred cities worldwide. This anger combines with a grievance against the crisis of democracy: as the Spanish Indignados put it, "We have a vote, but not a voice." In her analysis of financialized capitalism, Nancy Fraser has pointed out that capitalism's drive to endless accumulation tends to destabilize the very public power on which it relies. This is now being experienced as a crisis of democracy, thus adding a political element to the inventory of capitalism's contradictions that ground its crisis tendencies (Fraser 2015). This would suggest the brewing of a crisis of the legitimacy of democratic capitalism as a social order. We should be expecting either massive popular mobilizations against capitalism or radical efforts on the part of ruling elites to reinvent it, akin to the concerted cross-ideological efforts that erected welfare capitalism.

And yet, social protest has not affected the policy consensus behind the logic and logistics of precarity capitalism. With the blessing of electorates, governments are busy enacting policy packages very similar to the ones that triggered the meltdown of 2007–2008. The economic nationalism that has taken the upper hand in Britain and the United States (via, for example, Brexit and the election of Donald Trump to the U.S. presidency) is a confirmation that the national competitiveness in the global economy remains a top policy priority. By all evidence, precarity capitalism relies on a potent source of legitimacy. What is it?

As I noted in the exposition of the theoretical framework in chapter 2, the legitimation of the social order is grounded on what publics perceive to be "political deliverables" within the legitimacy deal—functions that people not only deem *desirable*, but also *possible* for public authority to perform. It is this legitimacy deal, and the broader legitimation matrix (shared understandings about what is a fair distribution of life-chances in society) that has altered in such a way as to sustain capitalism in its new modality.

Since about the turn of the century, public authority at all levels of governance has undertaken ever more policy action to enhance market efficiency and intensify the production of wealth, including regulations enabling the commodification of risk and the extension of rentierism. This has entailed a dramatic increase in social risk, while the responsibility for the generated risk has been diffused. This is done under the dictum that, even if a social safety net remains politically desirable, it is economically unfeasible (as per the common narrative that increasing taxation would make companies relocate abroad, would be a disincentive to hiring, etc.). This means that a social safety net is no longer thought to be a "political deliverable." The legitimacy deal between citizens and public authority has effectively altered in such a way as to absolve the state from its primary social responsibility of maintaining a correlation between risk and opportunity, a key legitimation resource of democratic capitalism.

Let us examine this development in further detail. How is it possible that society gives its endorsement to a socially irresponsible rule that is so obviously detrimental to individuals, communities, and their natural environments? The answer lies in the recasting of the framework of political relevance within which the legitimacy deal between public authority and citizens takes shape. Under the grip of the survival-of-the-fittest functionalist logic of the TINA policy doctrine enacted by policy elites since the 1980s, economic reason substitutes for political reason. The *raison d'économie* does not just overtake the old *raison d'état*, putting it to its service, but replaces it.[20] This allows the social costs and effects of policy to be disregarded, since these policies are deemed to be without alternative; instead, social welfare is equated with national economic growth, itself predicated on competitiveness in the global economy. This remains true even when governments switch to economic protectionism—as is being attempted by President Trump. Helping specific companies or industries through protectionist trade policy does not alleviate the pressure on society as long as it is believed that public resources must be poured into global economic competition, which entails wage repression, insecure jobs, and underfunded public services.

As the *raison d'économie* subjects all social practices to the imperative of competitive profit production, the political economy of neoliberal capitalism, followed by that of precarity capitalism, gradually accomplishes what Wendy Brown has described (2015) as the thorough "economization" of society: the

economic logic of markets has penetrated our collective perceptions of fairness and personal visions of self-worth. Economistic
logic has permeated all aspects of our lives: it has contaminated
statehood, the system of education, the courts, even the way we
think about and value ourselves and our lives. The tragedy is not
simply that the super-rich have hijacked democracy through
their wealth and an electoral system that predicates outcomes
on available cash. The situation is much darker: by endorsing an
economistic logic of success and failure, the demos disintegrates
into bits of human capital, as Brown puts it, while the state
itself actively produces voters as economic actors.

Let me illustrate this development with a highly celebrated
policy initiative in Europe. The "Horizon 2020" research and
innovation program of the EU has sharpened the focus on fostering partnerships between universities and private companies,
with the purpose of stimulating economic growth in Europe.[21]
This arrangement not only directs scientific research to projects
with immediately marketable outputs, but does so with public
funds. As private companies own the patents resulting from these
projects, they reap the opportunities for profitmaking while the
risks are offloaded to society. This is being justified with a narrative of increasing companies' competitiveness as well as job creation: the lack of innovative ideas on the market is allegedly due
to the high risks that companies take in financing scientific
experiments, so the EU underwrites this risk for them. On the
other hand, the direct involvement of companies allows them to
steer scientific research in a financially profitable direction, which
is presented as an obvious virtue of the program (EC 2011). One
of the unintended consequences that has come to the surface in
the implementation of these projects is that the participating
companies are more focused on the training and recruitment
of individual researchers (a brain-drain from the public to the

private sector) rather than in achieving stated scientific goals. This powerful framework of EU funding for market-oriented research has entailed what we might call the "financialization of academia," where academic promotions have become conditional on capacity to apply successfully for EU funding. The rampant commodification of knowledge and the erosion of the scientific rigor of research throughout Europe are not a casual collateral damage in the pursuit of society's well-being. The practice of redistributing advantage to those who can enhance economic competitiveness irreversibly alters the framework of meaning and valuation through which citizens relate to things such as knowledge and learning, academic achievement, and even personal merit. Significantly, no social protest has emerged against these shifts of policy, as they are perceived to be the only available course of policy action in the context of global market competition: remaining competitive is allegedly the only way to secure the public good. It is not so much the aspiration for scientific breakthrough and its potential contribution to long-term societal well-being that drive EU's research and innovation policy, but fear of losing the competition game in the global political economy.

Now that we have elucidated some of the motivational resources of precarity capitalism, it is worth taking a longer view of the main shifts that have taken place in the life and times of democratic capitalism. In the first format, the liberal capitalism of the nineteenth century, control over market forces remained with the individual, who was "free" to reap the gains of participation in the game of competitive pursuit of profit, as well as to shoulder the costs of failure. This purported control over one's destiny—an ideal coined by the Enlightenment—supplied the motivational energies to capitalism in its early life. In the second stage of capitalism, the welfare capitalism of the early and mid-twentieth century, control shifted with the state and the bureaucratic hierarchies. The repression of individual initiative was amply compensated for by the ideals of inclusive prosperity, engendering a consumerist hedonism as the driving motivational force. Under the neoliberal capitalism of the last two decades of the twentieth century, control over the distribution of economic opportunities and risks shifted from the state to the managers of globalization: multinational corporations and the leadership of the international financial institutions and the WTO. In the novel context of precarity capitalism, the shifting of risk to society, combined with the ever-growing complexity of production networks and value chains, creates an unmanageable complexity. Nobody has a clue where to begin to address the challenges, and events take over. The singular motivational resource is fear at personal, group, and institutional levels. Desperation is the raw material capitalism now feeds off, as Peter Fleming pointedly observes (2017, 25).

This fear is also affecting the nature of social protest. Let us turn to this next.

THE POLITICS OF PROTEST

As noted, economic rationality has permeated all social practices. This has made it possible for the new redistributive policies under precarity capitalism (from society to select economic actors, from the poor to the rich, from the weak to the powerful) to be accepted with so little resistance from society. However, I will steer away from the verdict of the death of democracy (Keane 2009). The lifespan of neoliberal and precarity capitalism has been rich with vigorous civil society mobilization on such issues as gender parity, racial equality, LGBTQ rights, and environmental protests. Moreover, these have had a tangible and irreversible effect on policy, belying complaints that social protest has become politically impotent (Lilla 2016, 2017; Hardt and Negri 2017; Tufekci 2017; Srnicek and Williams 2015; Roberts 2013). The massive protest movements that initiated the Arab Spring in 2010–2011 achieved nothing short of regime change, even where they failed to realize their aspirations for liberal and socially responsible rule. In Brazil, the nationwide anticorruption demonstrations in 2013 empowered then-President Dilma Rousseff, in the face of fierce opposition from political and business elites, to fast-track laws enabling the independence of the judiciary. This unraveled a global network of business and political graft through an investigation of the Petrobras company ("Operation Car Wash") launched in 2014. Protest movements have successfully affected the political process in Western liberal democracies, even on highly specialized matters such as technology, considered to be the exclusive purview of scientific technical elites (Feenberg 2017).[22]

It would therefore be implausible to argue that the TINA policy consensus among center-left and center-right political elites and the bureaucratic mechanisms of its execution have eliminated politics and democracy altogether. It is not the impotency of protest politics that distinguishes our predicament. It is true that many of the insurgencies have failed to change the course of policy, despite impressive mobilization. This has been particularly true of what Zeynep Tufekci (2017) has named "adhocracy," the spontaneous mobilizations enabled by information technology, and the petitions, occupations, strikes, vanguard parties, and affinity groups Nick Srnicek and Alex Williams (2015) have dismissed as "folk politics." It also seems to be true about the Yellow Vests in France, who have demonstrated, at times violently, for months on end. The government has responded to their grievances about high costs of living with further tax cuts rather than by strengthening the social safety net, allegedly for the sake of keeping the French economy competitive in global markets.

It might be true that the networked protests in our digital age lack the organizational rigor of the postwar civil rights movement, whose leadership and strategy had enabled them to affect the policy process directly. However, even when incapable of transforming policy, social protest is still fulfilling its core function: to frame the agenda of political debate by making grievances of suffered injustice relevant to politics. Prominent mobilizations such as the Occupy movements of 2011–2012, the Black Lives Matter demonstrations in 2014, the 2003 protests by millions of people in more than sixty countries against the prospect of war in Iraq, and the Women's March in January 2017 may not have affected the course of politics, but they did change the public narrative: that is, they altered the framework of political reference. Before Occupy propelled inequality to the very center of discussions of justice in the United States, the notion had been at the margins of the political agenda. It would be indeed a sign of the poor health of liberal democracy if we are to expect civil society to rival political society and do its work. It is the division of labor between civil and political society, between street protest and party politics, that fuels the vitality of modern democracy.[23]

The deficiency of social protest and political mobilization in the early twenty-first century lies elsewhere. Social harm incurred by the imperative of competitiveness in the global capitalist economy has exited the framework of political reference; it has left the agenda of public debate, and thus stands beyond the scope of political contestation. Politics is not dead. In Europe, disagreements persist over the benefits of remaining in the EU; in the

United States, over gay marriage, abortion, health care, and the need to extend U.S. military involvement abroad. What has happened is that the space of politicization has *contracted*, shrunk.[24] Until recently, social harm generated by the combination of free market policies and global market integration stood outside the space of political contestation because the social impact of such policies dropped out of the legitimacy deal between citizens and public authority. This is evidenced in, for instance, analyses establishing that globalization weakens the connection between the national economy and citizens' political choice. Economic openness reduces voter tendencies to hold incumbent policymakers responsible for economic performance and, by default, for the social consequences of economic policies (Hellwig and Samuels 2007).

On the left, it has become fashionable to talk about shared social responsibility (an idea that emerged around the turn of the century), as well as to appeal for the state to give power and resources directly to the people. The Left is not only failing to mount an opposition and propose a macro alternative, but it is compounding the problem with positions that, strangely, echo a neoliberal discourse of antistatism, thus further absolving political elites and public authority of obligations to rule in the public interest. In the current context, appeals for "more democracy" have become part of the problem, even as they are presented as radical solutions.

How about the upsurge of populism, with its calls against globalization? Isn't this, as many have argued, a sign that neoliberalism is finally in crisis? With the exception of the few instances of what is now labelled "left populism" (a term I rejected in the previous chapter), as expressed by the rise of the Syriza party in Greece and Podemos in Spain and support for presidential candidate Bernie Sanders in the United States, the rise of populism has at best aided neoliberalism to deteriorate into precarity capitalism. Antiestablishment mobilizations have targeted global market integration and its attendant cosmopolitan culture, not the neoliberal domestic policy formula of deregulation and liberalization of product and labor markets. The calls are to shut the door on immigrants and imports, not to end socially disembedded capitalism.

In sum: there hasn't been a legitimacy crisis even at the nadir of the economic meltdown in advanced liberal democracies because the legitimacy deal between citizens and public authority has come to exclude issues of social safety. At the same time, the larger legitimation matrix (regarding the distribution of life-chances) has altered: issues of social justice have been redefined in terms of protection of cultural lifestyles within national borders. Public authority remains free to cause social harm, for which it does not assume responsibility because the very publics who are suffering the effects of economic policy have absolved it from responsibility for the social consequences of that policy. This deficiency of responsibility cannot be remedied easily with the tools of representative, participatory, or deliberative democracy, and even less so with those of the fragmented resistance, devolution, and poststructuralist ontologies of social empowerment.

It is not simply the alliance of center-left and center-right party elites and the electorates that propel them to public office who are the culprits for imposing "socially irresponsible rule." The radical Left and the Far Right have done their share in contracting the space of political contestation. Calls against inequality (from the left) and for safeguarding societies from troublesome incomers (from the right) share a particular logic: they help to politicize the social evils that globally integrated capitalism incurs in the terms of distribution of membership within a given social order. This prevents questioning the social order within which equality and inclusion are being sought. When social harm is thematized in terms of inclusion and equality, it misrepresents instances of what I labeled as *systemic* injustice in chapter 2 as *relational* injustice instead. In other words, problems of the model of well-being generated by the sociopolitical system are translated as problems of one's place or inclusion within it. This invites remedial policies of redistribution or inclusion/exclusion rather than radically altering the rules of the game. The most disturbing example of the fallacious politicization of otherwise valid social grievances is the recourse to xenophobia, where political actors have used the most easily available language of political mobilization—that of hatred—to cash in on social discontent.

With the exception of environmental protest, which does indeed target the overall logic of capital accumulation (the way goods are produced, distributed and consumed), the shared myopia across forms of social protest and intellectual critique involves focusing attention on instances of injustice rooted in the *asymmetrical distribution of economic, political, or symbolic power* among actors, a practice engendering inequalities and exclusion. The logical solution, then, is to equalize power relations through redistribution and inclusion, rather than alter the very logic of social reproduction. This inability to question the political economy of capitalism and the democratic framework of politics in terms other than distribution and inclusion persists. It is well illustrated by the Occupy movement and what are now considered radical calls for justice, such as "We Are the 99 Percent" and "Tax the Rich." While anger is rightly and poignantly mobilized against the uneven distribution of advantage in our societies, it leaves the mechanisms that produce advantage unquestioned—and the whole way of life sodden with injustice for all.

The elimination of power inequalities within a system of social relations is valuable in its own right, but such efforts have tended to divert attention away from forms of domination rooted in the operative logic of the social system beyond a concern with equality and inclusion within that system. This is not an unfortunate oversight that can be remedied easily. It is driven by a compelling logic: the insistence on inclusion and equality within a certain model of well-being gives that model validity and vigor. We have to value the world within which we seek inclusion and equality; the harder the struggle to achieve access and status within that world, the more we value it. In chapter 2, I referred to this conundrum as the "paradox of emancipation." By falling into the trap of the emancipation paradox, social protest and intellectual criticism inadvertently fortify the legitimacy of capitalism, without solving the social crisis. We remain trapped in the inflammatory condition I called "crisis of the crisis."

It is in this metamorphosis of the legitimacy relationship of current-day capitalist democracies that we find the key to the two paradoxes of the missing crisis of capitalism that I laid out in chapter 1. Capitalism avoids its legitimation crisis, even as it has violated the ground rule in its legitimation matrix of correlating social opportunities and risks. This is the case because the legitimacy deal—not despite, but through social protests—has gradually altered to exclude a robust social safety net. Social safety, even as it remains highly desirable, is no longer among the "political deliverables"—services public authority is required to deliver. By politicizing the roots of the crisis (e.g., a political economy that produces massive precariousness) into the frames of inequality and the menace of immigration, struggles against injustice are enabling the system not only to escape a legitimation crisis, but also to successfully co-opt the emancipatory energies of protest and thus regenerate itself. The pleading cry of the young Spanish Indignados—"We are not against the system, the system is against us"—was hardly a call for a revolution.

Liberal democracy might be as much part of the problem as it is part of the solution. To the extent that democratic politics is a matter of an institutionally mediated expression of largely shared preferences, it takes place on the terrain of an existing relationship between public authority and citizens—a legitimacy deal. Whatever is not part of that deal cannot be politicized and therefore cannot be challenged. If this relationship excludes social injustice and either precludes the formulation of certain social grievances addressed to the political authority or politicizes them in the wrong direction via the shortcut of xenophobia, the common instruments of democratic politics are unlikely to be of much use. The novel capital–labor alliance in favor of neoliberal globalization I discussed in chapter 3 blocks the capacity of electoral democracy to tackle the conundrum. This is not a matter of "false consciousness." The remarkable phenomenon of the twentieth century is not so much the rise of the real income of the working class, but the increase of labor's stake in the capitalist system, as Joseph Schumpeter observed in 1943 (310). Moreover, as Wolfgang Streeck (2014, 21) notes, "expectations in relation to which the political-economic system must legitimate itself exist not only among the population, but also on the side of capital-as-actor." In other words, the interests of capital, together with its main dynamic of competitive production of profit, have a legitimate place in a democratic political system. We cannot blame capitalism for eroding democracy and try to reverse that erosion with more democracy. What we need is less capitalism.

Moreover, since the rise of "shareholder democracy" in the late twentieth century, a large section of the population is both wage-dependent and profit-dependent, if only through the investment of pension savings in the stock market. Until recently, profit-dependent and wage-dependent interests were at loggerheads: capital interests result from income dependence on return on invested capital and therefore owners and managers of capital sought to maximize the yield from their investments, not least by repressing wages. Even as this still remains the case in principle, wage-dependent groups have developed an interest in the stability and growth of financial markets, either because this affects the availability of employment and therefore of livelihood or because they have become themselves to some extent profit-dependent by owning stocks through their pension funds. To the extent that the boundaries between these groups remain blurred, everyone's (immediate) welfare becomes dependent on the good economic health of capitalism, even when it can no longer ensure improving living standards or fair distribution of life-chances and is rampantly destroying the environment. We are all capitalists now—and the mechanisms of collective opinion and will formation (the media, education, deliberative fora) as well as the logistics of expressing the popular will (democratic elections) give voice to that uncomfortable truth.

If we are to transcend the current socioeconomic system, we can therefore rely neither on its terminal crisis nor on a popular revolution. There is no available utopia to guide such an effort, as I argued in the previous chapter. However, the possibility for overcoming capitalism has never been as attainable as in our times.

6

WHAT IS AILING
THE 99 PERCENT?

*I must study politics and war, that our sons may have liberty
to study mathematics and philosophy. Our sons ought to study
mathematics and philosophy, geography, natural history and
naval architecture, navigation, commerce and agriculture in
order to give their children a right to study painting, poetry,
music, architecture, statuary, tapestry and porcelain.*

—John Adams, in a letter to Abigail Adams, 1780

W e have established that the contemporary context
is void of utopia, revolution, and even a life-
threatening crisis of capitalism. The potential for
overcoming capitalism should be sought elsewhere. Unlike in
previous historical junctures, the current emancipatory opening
is triggered neither by troubles in capitalism's economic performance (as during the Great Depression of the 1930s) nor by
indignation at its poor distributive outcomes (impoverishment,
inequality, and exploitation engendering class war, as during
the mid-nineteenth-century upsurge of socialism). I will argue,
in what follows, that a countermovement against capitalism is
now being generated by another phenomenon: namely, that a

multiplicity of social groups across the capital–labor divide, irrespective of how they are affected by the distribution of social advantage and wealth, are aggrieved by capitalism's very constitutive dynamic—the competitive production of profit—even as productivity and economic growth are rising.

Let me begin from where we happen to be historically—a time of vocal social protests. The outrage against inequality ("tax the rich"), the demonization of greedy bankers (as if they would be doing their job if not trying to maximize profit), the protests against austerity (implying an entitlement to affluence), the calls for exclusion of immigrants (as these "desperate people" menace the social peace) all signal, in various ways, a longing for the "roaring nineties," before the financial meltdown of 2007–2008, before the sense of physical insecurity unleashed by 9/11, before the migration "crisis" of 2015. Yet this was a time when neoliberal capitalism was preparing the economic and social disasters of the early twenty-first century, intensifying the drive for competitive profit production at the expense of human beings and nature.

Left-wing political forces are now mobilizing for the recovery of democracy by way of radical equality, hoping for the return of the inclusive prosperity that existed under welfare capitalism, which neoliberal capitalism all but eradicated. The Party of the European Socialists (the center-left group of the European Parliament) built its platform for the May 2019 elections on "Eight Resolutions for Equal Society" in a nostalgic gesture to the welfare state. However, it was this inclusive prosperity—based on enhanced consumerism—that drove production and job creation, which wrecked the environment.

Much present-day social protest and political mobilization is defensive, nostalgic, or conservative in nature; some of it is even reactionary. Yet, as per the formula of critique I elaborated in chapter 2, it all supplies valid points of entry into the larger story of social injustice, points from which the search is to commence for the origin of these grievances in the structural contradictions and constitutive dynamics of capitalism. I proposed that normative critique and strategies of emancipation should emerge from an analysis of the mechanism that translates structural dynamics at work on the level of political economy into politically salient social concerns with injustice.

According to the algorithm of analysis I adumbrated, we are to proceed as follows: Taking a perceived pathology as a symptom that something is amiss, we seek to identify those antinomies (internal contradictions) of contemporary capitalism that foster *historically particular* but *structurally general* experiences of injustice, and from which *normatively generalizable* notions of justice can be derived, then set political goals accordingly. This allows visions of social justice to emerge from the identification of a broad pattern of societal injustice, surpassing the grievances of particular groups while addressing all of them. I will now deploy this formula in an analysis of contemporary liberal democracies and the opportunities for emancipation that the current historical conjuncture contains.

In chapter 3, I discussed the rise of xenophobia in Europe and the United States. Its pathological nature is shaped from three directions: (1) in terms of wealth, infrastructure, and political know-how, our societies have an unprecedented capacity to accommodate the increased but relatively weak influx of asylum-seekers and economic immigrants, yet many still believe that the arrivals pose a threat; (2) the parties expressing anti-immigrant sentiment are often culturally liberal; (3) there is a discrepancy between xenophobia's economic nature, driven by fears of loss of livelihood, and its noneconomic roots: anti-immigrant mobilizations began well before the economic crisis and spread mostly in the affluent societies of northern Europe.

Rather than discarding these populist mobilizations as malignant, I discussed them in chapter 3 as expressions of a thorough reshaping of the ideological map of the mature capitalist democracies. This is driven by a new set of concerns: physical insecurity, political disorder, cultural estrangement, and employment insecurity, which I described as the four ingredients of a new order-and-security agenda. It is on the basis of this that the former extremes of the left–right axis of political competition are now converging into a "risk" pole. Thus, what many people perceive to be the key pathology of our societies—rising xenophobia—is a symptom of broadly shared fears of loss of livelihoods, which I traced (in chapter 5) to the political economy and institutional logistics of what I described as "precarity capitalism," the model of democratic capitalism we currently inhabit. However, as ruling center-left and center-right elites continue to impose the neoliberal policy logic of economic liberalization, populist voices advocate the shortcuts of old solutions, from "keep foreigners out" to "tax the rich." These answers align with what I described as legitimate but short-sighted concerns with relational domination (inequality and exclusion). However, fixing inequality with a bit of redistribution rather than removing the engine of poverty and inequality produces what I described as the paradox of emancipation: even successful struggles against relational domination risk deepening systemic domination—the harm inflicted by the competitive production of profit. There is no legitimacy crisis of capitalism, as the very social protests that are meant to undermine it grant it a tacit endorsement. We seem to be stuck in a "crisis of the crisis of capitalism," with our efforts at crisis management (some redistribution, tightening migration controls, giving more direct power to the people via referenda and national debates) perpetuating the crisis. Where is the way out?

I will next proceed to screen the political economy of precarity capitalism and the types of social injustice it generates in order to discern available possibilities for radical transformation of the social system. Without implying that the economy is the basic and primary source of social injustice, I will draw attention to novel forms of immiseration that arise from the recent transformation of the political economy of advanced industrial democracies. We will see how from these diverse experiences of injustice social forces can arise with a common interest in overcoming capitalism. The emergence of these social forces, as well as the conditions for transcending capitalism, have to do with two structural contradictions (antinomies) of contemporary capitalism.

THE TWO ANTINOMIES OF CONTEMPORARY CAPITALISM

Precarity capitalism—the model that superseded the neoliberal capitalism of the late twentieth century—is the outcome of intensified global competition ("globalization") and the policy imperative of economic competitiveness. It was spurred by the combination of two principles of neoliberal economic policy: free markets and open economies. The deregulation of national economies and the opening of domestic markets through free trade generated a global capitalist economy organized on the principles of free markets. Thus, the laissez faire principle supplied the rules of the game of the global economy. The global political economy is rule-based. In principle, the integration of national markets can follow a multitude of patterns determined by the particular conditionality of trade and investment policy (conditions for importing goods and exporting capital). However, due to their leadership position in global market integration, the advanced capitalist democracies of Europe and the United States imposed on the global economy their own domestic model of neoliberal capitalism—a model centered on product and labor-market deregulation and privatization of public assets. This process of modelling the world economy on the blueprint of Western neoliberal capitalism took place mostly within the institutional framework of the World Trade Organization, founded at the zenith of the neoliberal 1990s.

Even as this global socioeconomic system is politically navigated via a variety of national political systems (from liberal democracies to Islamic theocracies) as well as international and supranational policy regimes (from the UN to the EU), the logic of ever-intensifying competitive pursuit of profit has come to permeate most social practices. As states assist a few handpicked companies, competitive pressures on the rest are intensifying, a notable feature of precarity capitalism.

I commented in the previous chapter that the stratified distribution of life-chances in this context concerns the institutionalized and state-managed distribution of risks and opportunities generated by the new economy of open borders and information technologies. Let us scrutinize this process further, now paying closer attention on the evolving definition of life-chances, as well as their distribution.

On the one hand, the new economy has increased opportunities for wealth creation. Information technology (IT) and access to cheap labor through open markets has intensified the pace and enlarged the scope of profit creation. The new wave of work automation enabled by IT has helped to increase productivity. At the same time, the proliferation of forms of property ownership and job tenure have multiplied both the sources of income and the entry points to the labor market. These opportunities have not been bestowed only on the highly skilled, but also on the underprivileged. For instance, the knowledge economy has improved women's status in advanced industrial democracies; notably, it has allowed single mothers the flexibility they need to combine child-rearing with a professional career. The idiosyncratic formula of employment created by Uber has given people from ethnic minority groups their chance for employment in European societies where xenophobic attitudes would otherwise be an obstacle.[1]

This pluralization of the opportunities for wealth creation, together with the spread of the automation of work, has also increased the *decommodification potential* of societies—that is, the potential for freeing ourselves from dependency on paid employment. Like Gøsta Esping-Andersen (who follows Claus Offe), I use the term "labor decommodification" in reference to the autonomy of human beings from economic production, which enables their liberation from market forces (Esping-Andersen 1990). Decommodification, based on people's capacity to exit the labor market without damage to their well-being is, therefore, a precondition for the individual autonomy and life of self-fulfillment that the Enlightenment conceived as an aspirational ideal.

The decommodification potential is related to the increase in options available to individuals for exiting the labor market due to, for example, the proliferation of sources of income outside of gainful employment (such as investment in equity rather than exclusive reliance on a salary, which eliminates the need to spend time in a productive activity), or flexible and limited employment that minimizes the time spent in a productive activity. However, in any social system where basic needs are satisfied through work and employment is a main source of income, there is a dynamic relationship between labor commodification and decommodification. This was first articulated by Claus Offe when he conceived of this pair of concepts in his analysis of the political power of wage labor: workers' capacity to exit the labor market (and thus assert pressure on their employers via blocking the production process) is predicated on these workers' capacity for being hired as well as their value as profit-generating employees (Offe 1984, 153–54). Offe deemed that it is these dynamics that increase the power of wage labor, but we can extend this logic into a broader notion of emancipation, beyond the conceptual constraints of class. A person's capacity to step out of the systemic logic of competitive production of profit is predicated on the ability to extract sufficient income from that process, as well as on the capacity to find an alternative source of livelihood. John Maynard Keynes observed the rapid formation of this decommodification potential in the 1930s, when he described the coming twenty-first century as "the age of leisure and of abundance" ([1930] 1963, 358–73). Indeed, in Western societies in the decade from 1975 to 1985, people's free time surpassed their working time; leisure became the dominant social time (Yonnet 1999).[2]

Keynes's optimistic predictions have been partially fulfilled. By fighting social precariousness through stabilizing the labor contract, raising wages, and limiting work hours, the welfare state created decommodified spaces as well as legal and institutional mechanisms of decommodification. This, in turn, increased the perceived value of leisure time and created stable expectations for its availability. The information technology revolution of the late twentieth century and the massive automation of production it spurred "diminishes the amount of work needed—not just to subsist but to provide a decent life for all," as Paul Mason notes in *PostCapitalism* (2015), at least in principle, we might add. These changes in technologies and public preferences altered profoundly the shape and nature of the economy in capitalist democracies.

The "networked economy" (Castells 1996) of the late twentieth century replaced the rigid hierarchies and production practices typical of the Taylor-Ford model. This shift enabled a flexible career path, giving birth to what John Gray has described as the "portfolio person"—one without permanent attachment to any particular occupation or organization, whose skills allow for self-reliance in finding paid employment on his or her own terms (Gray 1998, 71–72, 111). This has not only increased a person's potential to control the time spent in paid employment, but also, as Gray notes, to engage in productive activity on one's own terms, which constitutes a form of emancipation. The portfolio person, relying exclusively on her own competence and performance, is free from the bureaucratic constraints and power dynamics of a career path within an organization. (Let us recall the leftist rejection of the welfare state on account of the bureaucratization of everyday life, a criticism also voiced by the youth protests of the late 1960s.) In other words, a person with a high capacity for voluntary entry into and exit from the labor market has the double advantage of being able to escape, even if temporarily, the burdens of productive employment, as well as to draw a maximum advantage from participating in it. (Institutional conditions permitting, that is. I will turn to this later.) My goal here is not to offer a detailed review of the intricate economic dynamics of our times,[3] but to highlight those of its elements that generate a decommodification potential—the material and psychological resources needed for one's exit from productive employment.

This expanding decommodification potential of our societies is one of the most significant ways in which opportunities have increased for both wealth creation and control over one's life. Not only are there greater technological and economic resources for decommodification (e.g., automation of work, flexible employment), but importantly, the social *value* of labor-market exit is tangibly on the rise: the importance of work-life balance and the value of discretionary time in general (beyond care responsibilities) is rising (Goodin et al. 2008; Inglehart 2008).

However, the information economy's liberating potential has failed to issue a novel economic paradigm along the lines of Paul Mason's "postcapitalism," which is marked by dramatically decreased time spent in paid employment and nonmarket forms of collaboration, exchange, and ownership, where economic activity is detached from the profit motive and products are instilled with a "moral interest" (Mason 2015). Commodification has, in fact, intensified and widened its scope due to advances in technology, in terms of both turning knowledge and risk into new fictitious commodities, as discussed in the previous chapter, and of increasing the time spent in paid employment. Today we can work from everywhere and at any time, and we do so. The decommodification potential of information technology has remained largely untapped.

Increased competition within deregulated and open markets has increased commodification pressures on labor, from expanding working hours and working lives, to the need for retraining in order to remain employable and the spilling over of work into leisure and domestic life. A survey of more than fifty countries by the ILO attests to a global trend in longer hours spent in paid employment (Lee, McCann, and Messenger 2007). Since its amendments in 2000 and 2003, the European Working Time Directive has allowed for longer working hours through voluntary opt-outs by employees from the weekly limit of forty-eight hours. As more bargaining power has been passed to lower institutional levels, recent changes in statutory legislation in

EU member states allow work schedules and work organization to be determined at the company or individual level, a practice that is associated with weaker compliance with working time standards and thus longer overtime. The gender difference in length of the workday has been slowly reducing, mainly because women, on average, are working more hours than before (Cabrita et al. 2016). Notwithstanding regulations, nonhourly workers across the world are commonly not paid overtime; they simply put in the hours for no extra compensation out of fear of losing their jobs.

These commodification pressures have been *generalized*: that is, they have expanded beyond paid employment and now encompass a multitude of groups. They now affect people in the workplace but also the unemployed and those at school—groups formally outside the labor market, but dependent for their subsistence on entry into the labor market and therefore focused exclusively on acquiring job skills and job-seeking. Significantly, the frequency of long working hours has increased rapidly among the top quintile of wage-earners (Kuhn and Lozano 2005). Thus, commodification pressures are affecting us all, from precarious and poorly paid workers to those in stable, well-remunerated employment, from the unemployed to university students. These pressures are transforming our lives into a perpetual effort of becoming and remaining employable.

The simultaneous increase of the decommodification potential of modern societies and the increase of commodification pressures constitute one of the key antinomies of contemporary capitalism. I will name this "surplus employability." This antinomy, in turn, affects the parameters in which social stratification and related forms of social injustice take shape.[4]

In the past, owners and managers of the means of production had a decisive advantage in the distribution of life-chances. Their social position secured them a privileged place in the process of capital accumulation. However, two peculiarities of contemporary capitalism alter this situation. On the one hand, as forms of ownership have proliferated and IT has reduced the cost of starting a business, ownership of the means of production has been democratized. This is particularly evident in the capacity of workers to hold stock equity in publicly listed companies. Thus pluralized and democratized, the ownership and management of the means of production can no longer provide a shelter against social evils such as economic insecurity and exploitation. On the other hand, competition in the globally integrated market has increased, even for the biggest companies, which means that the owners and managers of capital are more strongly subjected to competitive pressures, with all their negative effects. As a result, ownership of the means of production is no longer the structure that affects significantly the formation and distribution of life-chances in society. Instead, under contemporary democratic capitalism, it is the uneven distribution of society's decommodification capacities and pressures that has become the key logic of stratification. Those who can enter and exit the labor market at will are the winners in the distribution of social opportunity and risk.

The growing relevancy of labor-market access is due largely to the nature of state–market relations characteristic of democratic capitalism in the late twentieth and early twenty-first centuries. As I noted in the previous chapter, global economic integration has made competitiveness in the global economy, rather than merely growth or maintaining competition in the domestic market, a priority in economic policy. Maintaining competitiveness, however, does not condition growth on employment—indeed, the dominant formula since the 1990s has been that of "jobless growth," as well as "jobless recovery" from economic crises. The visibility of this phenomenon has been obscured by the recent proliferation of "nonstandard" (precarious and poorly paid) employment. The phenomenon of jobless growth effectively diminishes the pressure for wealth redistribution, as growth ceases to be seen as contingent upon full employment and domestic consumption but, instead, upon companies' successfully competing in the global economy, deriving revenue from global markets.

Remedial policies of wealth redistribution have been reduced since the late twentieth century (allegedly due to states lacking the financial resources). New stratification dynamics now center on access to earning opportunities. Thus, even as leisure has become an important component of the definition of a valued life, one's ability to access the labor market becomes a powerful factor in the distribution of life-chances. As Peter Fleming remarks, "for those of us who are not part of the global elite or transnational criminal class, paid work is the only way to obtain money" (2017, 30). Consequently, the institutionalized distribution of access to the labor market has become the major arena of social conflict. Notice how long-term unemployment among young people, especially in southern European countries, has become a major source of social discontent, as in the example of the Indignados in Spain who claimed their right to be commodified, so to speak, as a matter of a right to a decent life. In this new context, employment is no longer an element of *economic* policy as it had been in the growth-and-employment formula of welfare capitalism. Employment, rather, is a good to be distributed—an element of *social* policy. We might recall that during the global financial crisis, many European states endeavored to subsidize, via payments to employers, the maintenance of jobs that would otherwise have been shed. Such policies were meant not so much to revive growth (and often were criticized for preventing a return to growth) but to prevent unemployment as a source of social destitution.

Burgeoning research in recent years on the "winners" and "losers" of globalization in advanced industrial societies offers evidence of the increasingly stratified distribution of the opportunities and risks associated with access to the labor market and the particular positioning within it. The two groups are often cast in terms of the growing income gap between low-skilled and highly skilled workers in industries exposed to globalization (Geishecker and Görg 2007; Kapstein 2000). However, in view of the central antinomy of capitalism articulated earlier, in respect to the distribution of the decommodification potential and commodification pressures, social stratification occurs not simply in terms of access to the labor market, but also in terms of capacity for exit from it. This particular kind of labor market mobility determines whether globalization's risks translate as opportunities for increased wealth and autonomy (for control of one's life trajectory), or hazards. It is also associated with a successful lifestyle, one of maximum capacity for personal choice and availability of resources to achieve it.

This leads us to discern the second structural contradiction of contemporary capitalism. On the one hand, the thinning of the social safety net resulting from policies of austerity that were undertaken well before the 2008 financial crisis has increased a person's need to rely on employment because the sources of revenue that had been available under welfare capitalism are no longer there. On the other hand, the economy does not produce enough good jobs. The sources of this deficiency are three. First, automation is eliminating more employment than it is creating, and is beginning to replace not only routine blue-collar jobs, but also good, stable jobs that have been the foundation of middle-class prosperity in high-wage economies (Baldwin 2019). Second, in Western democracies, as public authority focuses on achieving competitiveness in the global economy, competition with capitalist dictatorships like China is putting pressures on remuneration, employment stability, and job availability. Third, democratic states are increasingly adopting as their main job creation strategy the sponsoring of economic "champions" (firms such as Airbus, Samsung, and Michelin). These companies are indeed reaping the financial benefits of the access to global markets. However, their production chains (and therefore, employment networks) span the global economy. The employment they create at home is negligible compared to that they create abroad.

With a thinner social safety net, our livelihoods are increasingly reliant on gainful employment, yet domestic economies are increasingly unable to provide it. This trend is global and the economic recovery of the postcrisis decade has not reversed it. According to the Director-General of the International Labour Organization, despite the stabilization of the global unemployment rate in 2017, "decent work deficits remain widespread: the global economy is still not creating enough jobs" (ILO 2018b). This deepened reliance on holding a job within a political economy that does not produce enough of them is the second contradiction of precarity capitalism. Let us call it "acute job dependency." It complements the first contradiction, "surplus employability"— the tension between the growing decommodification capacity and increased commodification pressures in Western societies.

Combined, the two antinomies have resulted in commodification dynamics permeating areas of our lives that were previously untouched by the productivist logic of capitalism. The "uberization" of the economy is a testament to this. Companies such as Uber and Airbnb were initially set up as income-generating sources allowing employment entirely on one's own terms.

Under the pressures of commodification within an economy that does not create reliable employment, these supplementary income–generating activities for which one uses one's personal property (a car, a home) have become a main source of livelihood. Nonproductive times and spaces have been transformed into revenue-generating sources; for many people, they are an exclusive, if highly precarious, source of revenue. Employment precariousness now afflicts skilled and highly educated workers as well, whose contracts are increasingly "nonstandard" and their unemployment benefits shrinking. This means that not only the unemployed but also the employed, and even the insiders of the labor market who are so envied, are on a permanent lookout for a job. We are all trapped in intensifying competition for fewer and fewer jobs, with our free time (an increasingly valued good) spent on building skills for finding a job and remaining employed and employable. From drinking our carrot juice to projecting the right image on social media, it is all for the sake of being marketable. This adds a layer of commodification pressures on top of the standard ones related to being in secure paid employment.

Strategies for coping with the Great Recession have in fact aggravated the situation: they have not solved the crisis, but instead normalized it into a condition I described earlier as "crisis of the crisis." Even as the economic and financial crises have been overcome, the social malaise persists into a condition of chronic inflammation. Its most tangible expressions are the long-term unemployment of young people and the proliferation of precarious and poorly paid employment even as unemployment rates are going down. Unemployment in the United States and Europe is being replaced by "underemployment," where workers have poorly paid part-time jobs and cannot make enough money to meet their needs while encountering wage-dampening in conditions of full employment (Bell and Blanchflower 2018; Mascherini 2017). While unemployment in the United Kingdom in spring 2018 fell to a forty-year low, the number of zero-hours contracts there—under which employers are not obliged to provide any minimum working hours and employees are not obliged to accept any work offered—has remained unchanged (Jackson 2018). These contracts were introduced in Europe and North America as a stopgap, a last alternative to unemployment. By all evidence, they have become a fixture of the postcrisis new normal.

THE SOCIAL QUESTION OF OUR TIMES

In the heyday of both nineteenth-century liberal capitalism and post-WWII welfare capitalism, the social question stood in terms of the poverty of wage labor. This type of injustice is entirely within the logic of relational domination: the domination of one group over others by force of the unequal distribution of resources (in this case, income). Social justice was therefore pursued through income substitution measures (wealth distribution), improvement in working conditions, and the stabilization of the employment contract to ensure a secure stream of income. Under the welfare state arrangement, systemic injustice caused by the pressures of competitive profit production was also countered via decommodification measures such as limiting working hours, granting paid leave, and providing unemployment insurance.

However, under precarity capitalism, the picture of social injustice has altered. As a result of the changes in the stratification logic of capitalism, experiences of social injustice now emerge not only in terms of pay levels and working conditions, but also in reference to the increasingly uneven distribution of the economic opportunity and risk related to labor-market entry and exit in the context of global economic integration. Employment flexibility had already been a leading feature of neoliberal capitalism. The difference between *voluntary* and *involuntary* flexibility (temporary or part-time employment) has became a vital social distinction related to types of professional competency. Voluntary flexibility is marked not simply by higher levels of income but also by more diverse income sources, which in itself is a form of income security that facilitates decommodification. The opposite holds for involuntary temporary employment, which most often affects lower-skilled workers in sectors exposed to international competition. Here, involuntary job flexibility combines low and insecure incomes.

The distribution of life-chances begins to be strongly predicated on *personal control* over one's entry into and exit from the labor market. This capacity or lack thereof demarcates voluntary job flexibility (an opportunity), which neither jeopardizes access to income sources nor the availability of discretionary time, from involuntary flexibility (a hazard). Involuntary flexibility is a serious threat to income security and also to personal freedom: the search for employment erodes discretionary time and is therefore a form of commodification. Thus, the highly stratified distribution of social risk and opportunity through one's capacity to exit from and enter into the labor market has become the true social question of our times. This framework of the social question emerged in the time of neoliberal capitalism, the last two decades of the twentieth century, as information technology and policy shifts toward deregulation of labor markets created the conditions for employment flexibility. What has changed under precarity capitalism with its newly intensified competition, itself a result of the policy objective of national competitiveness in the global economy, is that only a tiny minority of workers can profit from voluntary employment flexibility. This has led to the generalization of the state of precarity beyond the remit of insecure, meaningless, and poorly paid jobs—beyond groups lacking material welfare and suffering social exclusion (in the common usage of the term "precarity").[5]

In his *The Precariat: The New Dangerous Class* (2011), Guy Standing foretold the emergence of a growing group of people whose lives are defined by their employment insecurity. Importantly, this condition has afflicted even labor-market insiders and spread to the professional classes. In *Squeezed: Why Our Families Can't Afford America* (2018), Alissa Quart tracks the lives of what she calls the "middle precariat," a professional class encompassing professors, nurses, administrators in middle management, caregivers, and lawyers, all struggling to cope with life in the "always on" economy. Peter Fleming's *The Death of Homo Economicus* draws a similar diagnosis of the professional classes as trapped in jobs that are a "theatre of cruelty," besotted with stress and mental illness. "If homo economicus today is obsessed with money," he writes, "then it's purely in the negative sense, of being kept up at night worrying about the kid's school fees and so forth" (Fleming 2017, 8). The destabilization of sources of livelihood and the increased competitive pressure on almost all preceded the financial crisis of 2008, and the situation has not improved with the postcrisis recovery. At this point the precariat has become the 99 percent. Our age is not that of a precarious class, but of a precarious multitude.

From this diagnosis of the social question, relevant experiences of injustice (socially induced suffering) emerge along three lines. First, with the incapacity of national economies to ensure full employment, the secure labor contract that was once an instrument for safeguarding social rights has become a source of social exclusion: it leaves large groups without a chance to enter the labor market. Second, intensified competition over the past two decades has increased commodification pressures on the insiders of the labor market, the holders of secure and well-paid jobs. Labor in Western societies has made a series of concessions to income *level* (for example, wage freezes) and accepted longer working hours, as well as longer working lives (delaying the retirement age) in the name of employment *security*. Thus, relative impoverishment (via declining incomes) has afflicted the insiders of the labor market. Moreover, for this group, work-related stress has increased. It affects about 20 percent of workers from the 27 EU member-states and represents one of the biggest health and safety challenges (ERO 2008; ETUI 2018).[6] The number of suicides attributed to work-related stress has been on the rise since well before the Great Recession; trade unions have been sounding warnings that the root of this is excessive isolation of workers due to high workloads and fierce competition (Ughetto 2008).[7]

Studies also suggest that perceived job insecurity has risen substantially among highly educated and well-paid individuals, prompting them to work longer than they would like (Kuhn and Lozano 2005). Data from the European Social Survey indicate that skilled professionals report the highest levels of work–life conflict due to pressure from stressful jobs (McGinnity and Calvert 2009). Increased commodification pressures, especially working overtime, are particularly heavy on skilled labor in sectors exposed to globalization, notwithstanding the temporary reduction of working hours and wages, introduced as measures to save jobs in reaction to the 2007–2008 global financial crisis and resulting economic recession. Here, perceptions of economic insecurity act as a disincentive for voluntary labor-market exit even when such an exit is a highly desired option. Remaining fully employed becomes a form of social insurance. A 2015 survey of U.S. individuals with a net worth of over one million dollars found that, while 87 percent of those interviewed would rather quit the treadmill in favor of other pursuits, they remain at work out of an "ever-present fear of losing it all" (UBS 2015, 2).[8] The same study reports that three out of four millionaires in the United States consider themselves part of the 99 percent rather than the 1 percent, and are concerned that upward mobility is on the decline, expressed in personal anxiety about the future of their grandchildren. That would have equally befuddled Marx and Keynes.

The third line along which experiences of socially induced injustice emerge is the existence of a group on the margins of the labor-market: workers in temporary employment on an involuntary basis, especially in sectors exposed to globalization. Employment for unskilled workers in these sectors is marked by precarious and poorly paid jobs. This means that socially induced injustice of common genesis (i.e., related to the key antinomies of contemporary capitalism we traced earlier) has been generalized to include three large groups: labor-market insiders, labor-market outsiders, and people functioning on the margins of the labor market. The pracarization of society is complete.

To sum up the argument so far: Since at least the turn of the new century, we have inhabited a political economy marked by three peculiarities. First, the economy does not produce enough jobs: from well before the 2008 economic meltdown until a decade after it, Western societies experienced jobless growth due to automation of work and job outsourcing to areas with cheaper labor. Second, labor-market liberalization has reduced the security of employment—the so-called uberization of jobs. Thus, even when it is available, employment is no longer a reliable source of livelihood. This rather recent development has increased economic insecurity to unprecedented levels and afflicted almost all sectors of the economy, cutting across the capital–labor divide. The situation is aggravated by a third feature: public authority has been cutting social spending and thinning out the social safety net, a practice that predates the meltdown, but has intensified under postcrisis pressures to balance national budgets. Overall, this has engendered unprecedented economic uncertainty. The social question of our time is not growing inequality—it is the massification of precarity.

THE NASCENT ALLIANCE AGAINST CAPITALISM

In seeking a subject capable of resisting the global postnational systems of power, a subject also capable of creative political self-determination, Antonio Negri and Michael Hardt have adopted Spinoza's notion of the "multitude." In contrast to other types of collective subjects, such as the people, the masses, and the working class, the multitude does not possess internal coherence and has no clear boundaries; it is a complex subject "composed potentially of all the diverse figures of social production" (Hardt and Negri 2004, 2). My theoretical framework, centering on key antinomies of contemporary capitalism and three trajectories of domination, allows us to give tangible substance to the multitude as an agent of radical social change and the available paths of emancipation.

As noted, the structural contradictions of contemporary capitalism arise in the tension between two opposing tendencies. On the one hand, there is the unprecedented emancipatory potential of the new economy of open borders and information technology, as well as the shared awareness across society of the possibility and desirability of exiting the treadmill. On the other hand, pressures to focus one's efforts on remaining employed and employable have increased. While experiences of injustice vary across income levels and types of employment, the common denominator is the acute, widely spread sense of *insecurity*, of precariousness regarding one's livelihood. In the effort to discern the emerging multitude of forces, let us review the forms of social injustice typical of contemporary capitalism along the three types of domination that have guided this analysis so far.

In a globally integrated "world of overlapping communities of fate," to borrow David Held's fortunate phrasing (2016, 5, 10), the distribution of life-chances is strongly stratified. This stratification does not follow only the familiar fault lines of center vs. periphery, capital vs. labor, skilled vs. unskilled labor. Injustice emerges along three trajectories:

1. *Relational forms of domination and injustice*: To recall, the relational dimension of domination is one rooted in the unequal distribution of power in society by force of the particular distribution of material and ideational resources, such as wealth or social recognition (chapter 2). In the contemporary form of capitalism, inequalities in wealth have increased, while as a result of the relative success of the struggle for civil rights, the maldistribution of recognition has diminished. A notable feature of precarity capitalism is the acute increase in the asymmetrical distribution of economic risks. This is largely due to the fact that public authority, for the sake of enhancing national competitiveness in the global market, has begun actively allocating opportunities for wealth creation to specific economic actors and transferring risks to other actors and to society at large (chapter 4). As noted, the stratified distribution of life-chances is now mainly a matter of unequal access to the labor market, as well as of the capacity for voluntary exit from it, in conditions when the political economy

does not produce the needed jobs. These clusters of relational forms of injustice create their respective social conflicts and "class enemies": the 1 percent super-rich versus the remaining 99 percent; the cultural minorities who are gaining status (women, African Americans, LGBTQ groups) versus those losing privilege (white male blue-collar workers); the working classes of Western societies versus those in Asia or those of Western Europe versus those of Central and Eastern Europe, as employment in conditions of free trade and technological innovation shifts eastward seeking cheaper labor. Importantly, a new alliance is forming between capital and labor in specific industries and companies *within* Western societies. Here, the conflict is between those businesses that profit and those that lose from exposure to the new economy.

2. *Systemic forms of domination and injustice*: These are rooted in the constitutive dynamic of the social system, namely the competitive pursuit of profit. The stake here is not how life-chances are distributed, but what is being valued as a life-chance, as a form of successful life and as an accomplished self. The most extensively studied victim of systemic domination is the natural environment, as the extractive and polluting dynamics of capitalism are inimical to nature. However, forms of injustice rooted in systemic domination have recently proliferated. Earlier I observed that a feature of contemporary (precarity) capitalism is not simply the *intensification* of commodification pressures in conditions of integrated national economies. Its distinctive feature, rather, is that pressures that had previously affected almost exclusively blue-collar workers now encompass the whole of society and penetrate all spheres of life. These pressures are *generalized*. Through the massive precariousness of employment, they now affect even highly skilled and well-remunerated professionals, including the owners and managers of capital. As discussed

earlier in this chapter, the global dynamics of competitive production of profit generate a variety of experiences of economic
and psychosocial suffering: from being entrapped in poverty
(rather than just being poorer in relation to others) to anxiety
about impending loss of livelihood, high work-related stress,
and damaged work–life balance. We should add here also the
harm global competition incurs to the political system of Western societies. As these compete for jobs, profits, and markets
with the highly efficient autocratic capitalism of the likes of
China, Turkey, and Russia, they are emulating those features of
autocratic capitalism that make it more competitive: technocratic rule committed to the pursuit of profit without regard to
the damage done to societies, nature, and human beings.

3. *Structure-related forms of injustice (structural domination)*:
These are generated by the particular social institutions that
underpin and enable competitive profit production, such as the
technocratic machinery that controls the ownership and management of capital in China, or the varieties of private property
and management of the means of production (including in publicly listed firms) in capitalist democracies. In the current context, the big winners are those who can exercise a rent type of
control such as a natural monopoly and thus exempt themselves
from the pressures of competition. Here, the "class enemies" are
a transnational capitalist elite controlling a few large corporations
versus a divided working class and small businesses exposed to
the vagaries of intensified competition. In the United States, the
structure of electoral campaign financing allows for the systemic imperative of the competitive production of profit to penetrate into the political system.

Two peculiarities of social protest are currently preventing the
emergence of an agent of change via a broad mobilization of

social forces against the most deleterious effects of capitalism. The first is that lines of social conflict have proliferated into a network of antagonisms: the Western working class against the global working class; poor versus rich; owners of competitive industries versus those of noncompetitive ones; holders of stable employment contracts versus perpetual job-seekers. This *networked antagonism* blocks the emergence of a distinct revolutionary subject with a coherent ideology (utopia) around which a countercapitalist hegemony could germinate.

The second obstacle concerns the way in which the social justice and environmental justice agendas have been politicized. Until recently, the former was problematized, politically, in terms of relational injustice: impoverishment (cost of living concerns), inequality, and exclusion. The latter has been approached by social movements as a matter of systemic injustice. Opposition took place against the pursuit of profit and the production–consumption nexus, for which capitalism has relied on rampant extraction of natural resources. Politically, such concerns long remained framed as "lifestyle issues," while social justice was presented as a more urgent "bread-and-butter" issue. That is why it has been difficult to forge a broad coalition in support of fighting poverty and inequality, on the one hand, and saving the environment, on the other: with limited national budgets, electorates prioritized the bread-and-butter concerns over those of lifestyle.

The conflict between the two agendas has altered. It has become clear both that global warming is accelerating (WMO 2019) and that governments are not doing what is necessary to address the emergency. Only 16 out of the 197 signatories of the 2016 international Paris Agreement for action against climate change have adopted national climate action plans ambitious enough to meet their pledges (CRICC 2018).[9] This has altered the manner in which climate justice is politicized. The youth climate marches that took place across the globe in 2019 and the political action in support of the Green New Deal in the United States have reframed the environment as an "essentials of life" issue, linking it to the aggravation of poverty and a general threat to human life. This has increased the political significance of the environmental agenda. Positioning it on the same plane as issues of economic and social justice enables an alignment between the two agendas, which is a source of hope.

However, whatever rhetorical commitments to pursuing prosperity for all, as well as radical climate change, mitigation might be emerging; the conflict between the agenda of economic justice and that of environmental justice cannot be resolved in the current economic context of limited public funds, as investment in new technologies and raising the standard of living are both costly political objectives. In order to overcome this conflict and allow for policy action, a common denominator must bridge environmental concerns and issues of poverty alleviation. An overarching concern, a "chain of equivalence" (Laclau and Mouffe 1985), needs to emerge, linking the multiple struggles for emancipation into a common will aimed at the creation of what Antonio Gramsci called "expansive hegemony." To achieve this, Mouffe and Laclau proposed to reformulate the socialist project as "radicalization of democracy"—that is, to channel the energies of social protest into the building of a radical and plural democracy. Mouffe (2018) has reiterated this proposal, as the populist insurrections of the early twenty-first century triggered the crisis of the neoliberal hegemonic order. The idea of radical democracy captures well the current Zeitgeist of progressive political mobilization and academic scholarship, and it can indeed serve rhetorically as a much-needed wake-up call. I am skeptical, however, that more democracy can provide the logic of equivalence we need in the current historical situation. This is the case because the mechanisms of democratic decision-making, even when well deployed, tend to naturally prioritize short-term exigencies of justice (inclusionary growth) rather than the intangible, for many, reality of environmental devastation. Let us recall that, by ensuring a relatively inclusive prosperity, welfare capitalism inflated notions of basic needs and provided for their satisfaction through mass consumerism, which is reflected in pervading "democratic" expectations of what is deemed an acceptable standard of living (i.e., to be middle class and affluent).

We would need a more radical logic of equivalence, able to mobilize a multitude against all three core principles of capitalism: competition, profit, and production. Such a logic is available. It is located on the level of systemic injustice, where the enemies in the battles over relational and structural domination find a common front—namely, in their overarching discontent with the tangible effects of the competitive pressures of precarity capitalism. Such broad dissatisfaction with the constitutive dynamic of capitalism rather than with the inequalities and exclusions it creates (the triggers of anticapitalist mobilizations until recently) is without precedent. This creates a unique historical opportunity. Let us revisit this point in some detail, at the risk of repetition, as it is the kernel of the main claim of this book: namely, that conditions are now ripe for overcoming capitalism by subverting it from within.

The outrage of the 99 percent against the 1 percent seems to be voicing a protest against inequality as the main form of injustice of our times. Policy rhetoric, as well as some action across the left–right divide, has dutifully returned to ideas of redistribution. However, the changing nature of capitalism gives us reasons to read into these recent calls a concern that goes beyond inequality—a concern with a new form of social injustice, massive precarity, that is being mistakenly politicized in the easily available, familiar terms of inequality.

Danny Dorling (2015) is very much on target when he notes that, since the Great Recession hit in 2008, the rich have found new ways of protecting their wealth, while everyone else has suffered the penalties of austerity. Similarly, Anthony Atkinson (2015) notes that it is not simply that the rich are getting richer, but that the economy is rapidly changing and leaving the majority of people behind. If "leaving behind" is understood as actual or impending economic precarity rather than diminished consumption capacity, this is indeed a serious reason to be outraged. In 1859, Marx remarked that "there must be something rotten in the very core of a social system which increases its wealth without diminishing its misery" (1859b). A century and a half later, the spectacular increase in wealth is accompanied by a spectacular increase in forms of immiseration beyond economic impoverishment that are afflicting the multitude on both sides of the old class divide.

As we noted, the roots of social injustice in the current context have to do with a type of political economy that engenders generalized economic uncertainty, not simply inequality. This is an uncertainty to which almost all participants are subjected—apart from the top 1 percent, for whom obscene wealth is a source of economic and social safety. But this means that the type of inequality that generates social injustice is not so much inequality of wealth and income *levels* as it is inequality of wealth and income *security*, which in turn exacerbates the injustice of unevenly distributed social risks and opportunities. When we lack basic certainty regarding our source of livelihood, we lose control of our existence. Economic insecurity is politically debilitating; it directs all our efforts at finding and stabilizing sources of income, leaving neither space nor energy for engagement in larger battles about the kind of lives we want to live. "We are the 99 percent" does not express outrage against inequality of wealth, as it seems to do; it is, rather, outrage against disempowerment. It is not a cry for redistribution, but for regaining control. It is a call to end a system that thrives on taking control away from ordinary people. This is so because the systemic logic of capitalism—the competitive production of profit—has intensified sharply in the context of the "new economy" of open borders and technological innovation typical of the twenty-first century, while the policy responses to these pressures have engendered massive economic and social insecurity to which the 99 percent are subjected in numerous ways.

This understanding of the nature of social discontent and its sources allows us to discern a trajectory of change behind the thicket of seemingly disparate grievances and beyond the networked antagonism that pervades global capitalism. The spreading dynamic of social precariousness that afflicts almost all people fosters the formation of a very broad alliance of forces who share the desire (rather than a latent, unarticulated interest) to alter significantly the economic and political parameters of their societies. Despite the various forms it takes, social discontent in our times is shared by the winners and the losers in the uneven distribution of life-chances. At stake is not how life-chances are being distributed, but whether what is being pursued as a life-chance is desirable or even acceptable. It is the very definition of a life-chance as the successful participation in the competitive production of profit that aggrieves the multitude. This suggests that the possibility for a radical, if not revolutionary, change is now more obtainable than ever.

Every idea is only as strong as the social forces behind it. A potent social force is gathering behind the idea of overcoming the noxious competitive pressures of capitalism. These strange bedfellows include the proud rednecks of West Virginia, the IT engineers of Silicon Valley, the corporate lawyers of the City of London, and environmental activists in Brussels. We have come to a point in the development of democratic capitalism when the grievances voiced by a variety of social groups have to do with the systemic logic of capitalism—with the manner in which the competitive production of profit affects our lives, not simply with the unfair distribution of wealth. This gives us a chance to press for a radical transformation of the system even though, by all appearances, capitalism is doing very well. Capitalism may be in good health, but we do not need a crisis to embark on profound changes. These may seem unfeasible only to the extent that they are deemed unthinkable by the people at the steering wheel of politics. The next chapter surveys ideas that the majority of the 99 percent could propel into politics through already-available channels—from protest to elections and pressures on elite public opinion—thereby overcoming capitalism without the help of crisis, revolution, or utopia.

7

GETTING UNSTUCK

Overcoming Capitalism Without Crisis, Revolution, or Utopia

To be radical is to grasp things by the root.

—Karl Marx, "A Contribution to the Critique of Hegel's Philosophy
of Right" (1844)

The majority of young adults in the United States reject both capitalism and socialism, and young Europeans would join an impending uprising against the status quo, according to 2016 surveys.[1] European countries in 2019 were swept by high school students demanding gravely and persistently, week after week, urgent policy action on climate change, declaring our entire model of living to be pernicious. The young generation in Western liberal democracies demands a radical alternative and our times are indeed ripe for it. Uninhibited by old ideological truths, they are giving a voice to an overarching interest in transcending the existing system. How should these impulses translate into political mobilization and policy action? The past offers no solutions. As Nancy Fraser writes, "there is no going back to hierarchical, exclusionary, communitarian understandings of social protection, whose innocence has been forever shattered, and justly so. Henceforth, no protection without emancipation" (2013, 131). What would the road of emancipation look like?

Against forecasts that contemporary capitalism is about to crumble under its own weight, I claimed that although it seems to be coping fine with its economic and technological challenges, a potential for freedom from the pressures of competitive production of profit is growing within our societies. As I advanced in the previous chapter, there is now an emancipatory political force, a tangible and concrete multitude who could use the institutions of democratic politics to translate its discontents into policy. This would enable a significant, yet gradual metamorphosis of the social order, a process the Italian thinker Antonio Gramsci described as a "passive revolution." This chapter will address policies that would amount to such a radical overcoming of capitalism—policies that strike at the very logic of competitive production of profit.

Formulas for emancipatory political action span the expedient to the morally ambitious. Many of the advised and attempted policy solutions for dealing with the recent crisis have been in the range of the expedient—in the style of what Barack Obama in 2009 called "common-sense practical solutions to the problems we face." Exactly because they have been common-sense solutions, they are reactive crisis-management undertakings that, while providing emergency fixes to the ailing system, have unwittingly institutionalized the crisis, thereby perpetuating it—a situation I named a "crisis of crisis." Despite a return to economic growth, we are unable to exit the crisis because its root causes have been institutionalized into a new normal.

If the road of common-sense expediency is therefore a dead end, how about the road of the morally ambitious? The indignation against inequality, against greedy bankers and corrupt politicians that has enflamed public protest in the late 2010s is driven by such an ethical take on politics. This has energized political struggles for inclusive prosperity as a matter of economic and social justice. However, science and civic activism keep reminding us that it is exactly the "growing of the pie" that is destroying the very conditions for humanity's continuous existence on earth. Prosperity for all will destroy the planet.

If neither the politically expedient nor the morally ambitious would quite do, the solution, I suggest, must be located in a space in between: the field of what we might call the "politically hopeful." Hope, in contrast to optimism, as playwright-president-dissident Václav Havel has observed, "is not the conviction that something will turn out well, but the certainty that something makes sense, regardless of how it turns out" ([1986] 1991, 123). What is it that makes sense to be done, then, in terms of the analysis of contemporary capitalism and the nascent conditions for overcoming it, as laid out in the previous chapters?

Within the logic of analysis I have followed so far, which is driven by a commitment to emancipation from oppressive social dynamics rather than an abstract telos of, say, freedom or equality, policy action and social practice should target the three trajectories of domination along which social injustice emerges—the relational, structural, and systemic ones (see chapters 2 and 5). Let me address them in turn.

Along the first trajectory, unequal distribution of power among groups can entail the oppression (*relational domination*) of one group over another, resulting in social harms such as inequality and poverty. The injustice of these conditions does not stem from the moral desirability of equality and affluence. Moreover, inequality of wealth and income has been a long-lasting feature of capitalist societies without provoking much discontent; this suggests that citizens of these societies have viewed inequality as legitimate, even as some of their prominent moral philosophers have repudiated it as unjust. The rather recent outrage against inequality in Europe and the United States signals that the current state of inequality has become unjustifiable because it engenders unacceptable political and social privilege.[2] It is in this sense that economic inequality is a valid social concern.

The damage inequality incurs on social integration (due to, for example, a sense of unfairness or decreased trust in the government, the market, and other key social institutions) has been well-recorded in academic and policy research. I will not delve into this discussion. The effect on political agency deserves particular attention, as inequality in political influence is unacceptable from the point of view of what I described in chapter 2 as the "legitimation matrix" of liberal democracy as a political system—namely, equality of citizenship within collective self-determination.

Recent research has demonstrated that policymaking in the United States is dominated by powerful business organizations and a small number of affluent Americans, who exercise their influence throughout the electoral cycle largely via the mechanisms of campaign financing. As a result, policy reflects almost exclusively the preferences of the affluent (Gilens 2014; Gilens and Page 2014). Even if the particular enabling mechanisms of campaign financing are missing, as in most European societies, the thesis that citizens are not politically equal in economically unequal liberal democracies stands. Liberal values such as entrepreneurship and freedom of association foreground citizens' right to seek to influence policy; available material resources (money) and ideational resources (education) enhance the capacity for organized action and reasoned argumentation. Thus, competition among interest groups for political influence in economically unequal societies invariably creates a vicious circle. Economic inequality generates political inequality, which in turn reproduces economic inequality: economic inequality and political inequality are thus mutually reinforcing (Przeworski 2012).

It is well-documented that poor people are less likely to vote, whether due to lack of education or mistrust in the political system.[3] However, the problem of poverty's damaging effect on political agency has even deeper roots. In *Evicted* (2016), Matthew Desmond observes that poverty is politically debilitating. The tenants whose life he depicts are afraid to complain and lack any form of legal representation. Moreover, he notes, poverty is not an undesirable side effect of a system that creates welfare for all—it is a lucrative business; it drives capitalism. Therefore, redistribution for the sake of poverty alleviation and equalization of resources for political influence can have a transformative (rather than stabilizing, as many argue) effect on capitalism. Taxing the rich is a good place to start.

I also noted that relational injustice in the current context concerns the stratified distribution of labor-market entry and exit (chapter 6): those endowed with the right set of skills have the capacity to enter the labor market easily, hold a well-remunerated job, and exit at will. This is particularly important because the value of nonproductive time (leisure, family life) is on the increase and has become a salient component of the legitimation matrix of liberal democracies—the normative framework that specifies notions of life-chances and their fair distribution. Here, skill-building education and retraining—the favorite solution of well-meaning center-left and center-right policy elites—can be an effective means for equalizing life-chances.

We also need to tackle *structural domination*: injustices related to the structuring institutions that instantiate the dynamics of competitive profit production and competitive attainment of political office. With regard to the former, pride of place goes to the market as a mechanism of economic governance and the institution of private property and management of the means of production. In this regard, legislation aimed at reining in big corporations by giving workers and local communities a bigger say in the operation of the company (e.g., the Accountable Capitalism Act that Senator Elizabeth Warren introduced in the U.S. Congress in August 2018) would hamper, if not completely disable, the structural mechanism through which ownership generates economic power and political influence.[4]

In the contemporary context, a main structural source of injustice is that of rent-extracting oligopolies in sectors that are impervious to competition, such as electricity, gas, and broadband provision. By force of sector-specific resistance to competition, such companies need to be placed in public hands, even as they continue to be operated on market principles in determining the price of the service they deliver (as in the example of most railroad service in European countries and Amtrak in the United States).[5]

Structural injustice regarding the *political* system concerns the influence of money on politics, deployed via the institution of electoral politics. The mechanism of campaign financing allows (especially in the United States) the interests of economically powerful actors to hijack the decisional process. The strength of the U.S. political alliance between conservative and liberal elites in support of the revolving door between economics and politics is illustrated by the simple fact that European democracies are not as strongly afflicted by this malady. Paid political advertising on radio and television is forbidden in many European countries and campaign financing is allowed to a well-regulated minimum. If Americans generated the political will to block the impact of money on democratic politics, there is a reliable model near at hand to emulate. This is where public protest and policy action should start in the United States, as a matter of emergency. I will not dwell further on issues of structural injustice, as these have been amply covered in recent policy debates and academic research, from control on executive pay to breaking the market dominance of big tech, defying the influence of shareholders on the development strategies of publicly listed companies, and adopting communal forms of property.[6]

Above all, however, we need to, and can, target *systemic domination* via practices that oppose the competitive production of profit. This is the proper object of radical, revolutionary practice. I have already pointed out that it would not be sufficient to offer remedial solutions such as wealth redistribution to harm incurred by relational and structural domination. We need to focus our attention on the way the very constitutive dynamic of the system is instantiated in structural domination and expressed in relational domination. In other words, what is at the root of much of the suffering related to impoverishment, reckless management of the economy, political corruption, and environmental degradation is the competitive production of profit.

I have noted that our times are marked by an overarching, broadly shared injustice, one produced by competitive profit production: the generalized economic uncertainty that affects "the 99 percent." Herein lies the unprecedented potential our epoch contains for overcoming capitalism. Ever-intensifying competitive pressures forge systemic domination to which most members of society are subjected: that is, their lives are harmed by these dynamics. Many of the lucky winners in the uneven distribution of structural and relational power are also subjected to this systemic logic of capitalism and suffer its effects, from actual and feared job loss and impoverishment to work-related stress, mental health problems, and poor work–life balance. It is the distinct peculiarity of our times that both the underdogs (economically

exploited and socially excluded groups) and the purported winners in the game of competitive profit production (labor-market
insiders, owners and managers of productive assets) feel harmed
by these competitive pressures and are voicing their discontent.
Policy responses to these various grievances would inhibit the
very constitutive logic of capitalism—the competitive production of profit—and will result in a gradual exiting from this
system. In this sense, such policies and practices will be revolutionary. This will not, I contend, depend on a deliberate and
politically articulated endorsement of socialism or communism
as an alternative to capitalism. Such projects could motivate
radical action, but they are not a precondition for undertaking
anticapitalist radical practices. However, a problem with political agency arises.

I have claimed that the broad multitude's interest in opposing the dynamics of competitive profit production is not simply
an innate and latent one, akin to workers' interest in opposing
exploitation in Marxian analyses. This interest has become tangible in experiences of suffering and voiced in claims to injustice
as well as policy demands. However, uncertainty has a damaging effect on the *nature* of political agency. In conditions of
uncertainty, the creative energies of social discontent are trapped
by conservative instincts—it is fear that currently directs social
unrest into the reactionary path of xenophobia and autocratic
calls for law and order. Let us recall that the youth rebellions
that unleashed the bold social imagination of the late 1960s took
place on the back of two decades of stable prosperity. The men
and women who dared both dream and act were "bred in at least
modest comfort," in the account of one of their leaders (Hayden
1962, 45). This broadly shared prosperity and social stability marginalized the importance of bread-and-butter concerns and
shifted attention to postmaterialist values regarding identity,

freedom, and ecological justice.[7] These values were radicalized in the late 1960s into a youth protest against the consumerist lifestyles and autocratic values predominant under welfare capitalism.[8] Currently, young people dream about getting a job and spend their leisure on unpaid internships. "Sex, drugs, and rock and roll" are just song lyrics for them, not a slogan of a protest culture opposing consumerism and traditionalism.

Conditions of economic uncertainty—like the ones predominating now—trigger conservative instincts in support of the existing system. Paradoxically, this translates into clinging to the very dynamics that create general material and psychological precarity. Social unrest has been feeding on the sense of uncertainty fostered by the combination of globally integrated markets, technological upheaval, and vanishing social-safety nets. When faced with overwhelming risks, people start looking for an escape from the "freedom" of impossible self-reliance that has been forced on them. The conservative instincts that precarity has engendered feed into enduring electoral support to the center-right and novel support to the Far Right in the aftermath of the financial crisis. This is all the more surprising because the economic policies of privatization and deregulation that triggered the crisis, as well as the austerity measures used to manage it, were largely the brainchildren of the economically liberal right. However, the center-right has a reputation for economic expertise, especially the aptitude to navigate globalization, more so than the political Left. Thus, it is uncertainty, and the instinct it triggers in electorates for playing it safe, that motivates much of the center-right vote, while the antisystemic protest vote goes to the Far Right.

In this sense, the acute economic uncertainty that marks contemporary capitalism has a stabilizing effect on the system, even though it is detrimental not only to individuals and society, but to its very engine of prosperity, the market economy. It is often argued that inequality decreases consumption capacity, thereby hampering growth. However, economic and social precariousness (even in the absence of inequality or poverty) is also a strong disincentive to spend, be it to consume or to invest. Thus, economic insecurity is at the root of the struggle of the national economies in Western societies to return to their precrisis health. In conditions of economic uncertainty, providing cheap money to banks will not motivate them to lend. Nor will businesses with current account surplus rush to invest—they are either sitting on cash or using it to buy back their stocks to increase their value. In the same vein, the "project bonds" on which the European Union relies to generate the missing investment in large-scale infrastructure would not have the desired effect to encourage private companies to co-invest.[9] This means that, in the context of uncertainty, neither cheap credit, redistribution, nor labor-market deregulation alone would motivate consumers to spend and businesses to hire. In this sense, economic uncertainty is detrimental to the market economy, capitalism's engine of prosperity, even as the conservative political impulses it stirs up stabilize the political framework within which capitalism operates.

Paradoxically, therefore, the policy measures needed to spur the economic engine of capitalism are also those that provide the material conditions for political agency capable to oppose capitalism as a social system. Thus, in order to fight the systemic domination particular to contemporary capitalism and to prepare the socioeconomic conditions for transcending it, we need to build socioeconomic certainty—what I will proceed to describe as a "political economy of trust."[10]

The radical nature of this project stems from the fact that it counters the constitutive dynamic (operative logic) of capitalism, the competitive production of profit, while ensuring the material conditions of shared welfare. It does so by opposing the three elements of this constitutive dynamics: competition, profit and productivism (that is, the institutionalization of socially significant work as paid labor, deployed in a process of competitive production of profit). When these elements are eliminated, economic action and scientific activity can be directed toward the satisfaction of human needs. Recall that the profit motive spurs capitalism to create needs and then satisfy them, as discussed in chapter 2.

Policy measures targeting inequalities and exclusion (forms of relational domination), as well as those striking at structural injustices rooted in forms of ownership and management, are perfectly compatible with the operative logic of capitalism. For instance, the inclusion of women in the labor market has proven beneficial for capitalism, as it has increased the workforce and competition for available jobs and thus hampered the capacity of organized labor to obstruct the production process and press for higher pay and improved working conditions. Another typical measure of progressive politics, raising wages, improves purchasing power, thereby ensuring the consumption of commodities that is indispensable for a thriving capitalism. Such measures have a *stabilizing* effect on the economic dynamics of capitalism. They tame the system by feeding its constitutive dynamic, competitive profit production.

However, policies aiming to counter the competitive production of profit strike at the heart of capitalism, at its very operative logic. Pressures for such measures are accruing from a variety of directions. If enacted, in their totality they will constitute an *overcoming* of capitalism by subverting it from within. We do not need to define the shape of a postcapitalist society in order to endorse the logic of overcoming capitalism as a matter of the "politically hopeful"—of what makes sense in terms of tangible social dynamics and specific political demands.

The project I call a *political economy of trust* takes the form of a society that can satisfy human needs without devoting all of its energies to the process of needs satisfaction as capitalism does. (As noted, capitalism does this by perpetually inflating these needs as drivers of the generation of profit.) The "political economy of trust" policy platform pivots on the idea of preserving markets as a mechanism of exchange of goods and the private property of the means of production as one of the key structures of economic activity. However, the task of allocating productive inputs and social surplus will pertain not to the market, but to public authority. This will break the link between the market as a mechanism of exchange of goods and the process of competitive production of profit that allows private interest to trump public good. Although the private property of the means of production will allow for some competition among economic actors, this will be significantly limited because the mechanism of artificial creation of needs will be suspended. To achieve this, the political economy of trust has two components. The first regards global economic integration (globalization), the second, domestic social and economic policies.

1. *Recasting globalization*: Currently, the globally integrated economy consists not of national markets producing goods and exchanging them through free trade agreements, but of global production networks and value chains. This is why it is unfeasible or counterproductive to shut down a national market (e.g., by imposing tariffs on imports) in order to protect a national economy or even specific industries, as President Trump has been attempting to do.

As I noted, the creation of the globally integrated national markets in the late twentieth century took place, much under EU and U.S. leadership, on the terms of free (unregulated) markets. Eventually this unleashed the worst type of competition—the kind based on price—to the detriment of employment and environmental standards. The EU and the United States still have the chance to rewrite the rules of globalization by using nontariff barriers to enshrine in international law high standards of employment and remuneration, consumer protection, and care for the environment. Such standards define the best the transatlantic (Western) socioeconomic model has to offer: decent and dignified lives. The rest of the world will have no choice but to follow if it values access to the Euro-Atlantic economic space.

Why haven't we done this? At a point in recent history, we seemed to be on the verge of taking this path. The 2015 Paris Agreement on climate action would necessitate reshaping the global political economy exactly in this direction. In July 2018, the European Parliament adopted a resolution to make ratification and implementation of the Paris Agreement a condition for future trade agreements. This would have made it impossible to negotiate trade with the United States, which withdrew from the agreement in 2017. However, amid U.S. threats to slap tariffs on European car imports, in February 2019 the European Parliament overruled climate concerns to press ahead with U.S. talks. Altering the rules of the global political economy in a way to satisfy the exigencies of environmental protection and societal well-being would be costly for both consumers and businesses. Only a strong political leadership, backed by a broad, cross-ideological consensus of political forces, can override the short-term preferences of society in the manner in which most progressive achievements in Western societies have been made: from the rule of law to civil, social, and economic rights.

2. *Recasting domestic policy*: The second trajectory concerns domestic economic and social policy in liberal democracies. I have suggested that it is within the internal contradictions of contemporary capitalism that an emancipatory potential resides. Let us recall that the two key contradictions of precarity capitalism, as delineated in chapter 5, are (1) "surplus employability," the tension between, on the one hand, the increased value of discretionary time and the increased decommodification potential of modern societies, and, on the other, increased commodification pressures on everyone; and (2) "acute job dependency," the tension between decreased availability of jobs and increased reliance on a job as a source of livelihood. The potential for emancipation can therefore be activated via policy action aimed at designing a political economy that supplies secure sources of livelihood while allowing everyone to profit from the increased decommodification capacity of advanced modernity. Why is this the crux of social emancipation in our historical moment?

We observed that the institutionalized distribution of social opportunities and risks related to labor-market entry and exit (that is, the distribution of society's decommodification reserves and commodification pressures) has become a central mechanism of social stratification. One of the most salient axes of social conflict in our societies is the opposition between opportunities and capacities for voluntary entry and exit from the labor market versus being either an involuntary outsider to the labor market or being unable to exit it at will. Obtaining social justice in this context is, to a great extent, a matter of maximization of voluntary employment flexibility. This would allow creative human energies to be freed from the productivist imperatives of economic action driven by the profit motive.

Social justice, thus conceived, has an aggregative and a distributive aspect. The former concerns the overall *extent* of voluntariness in a given society, the latter the *equal distribution* of voluntary flexibility among participants. A just society would therefore be one with a high, widely spread combination of earning opportunity and capacity for decommodification: *voluntary* labor-market entry and exit. In other words, we need to mainstream (that is, both increase and allocate fairly) voluntary employment flexibility. I have called this a "universal minimum employment" platform (Azmanova 2012c), to complement the universal basic income platform and the building of robust public services.[11] This would imply breaking sector monopolies or providing some other measure of liberalization of labor markets to allow the outsiders to get in. On the other hand, we need a solid social safety net coupled with mandatory limitation of the time spent in gainful employment, to encourage voluntary exit from the labor market. This would entail the second step: a reform of social provision. Let me review each of these steps in some detail.

The distribution of economic opportunity and social risk is institutionally mediated. It is affected, for instance, by industrial and labor-market policies and by the nature of social provision, including whether this provision enables defamiliarization of care responsibilities. On an individual level, voluntary employment flexibility involves the combination of (1) one's access to gainful employment and (2) conditions enabling one's voluntary exit from the labor market, not least the unstigmatizing of such a withdrawal, if not putting a positive sanction on it. Voluntary flexibility is enabled when labor markets are sufficiently liberalized to allow outsiders to get in, while at the same time nonstandard employment is prevented from becoming precarious by regulating its terms (as is now done in the Netherlands, where part-time employment is highly regulated).

As noted in the previous chapter, in a context in which the political economy does not supply sufficient jobs, the liberalization of the labor market creates competitive pressures on participants. Regulated job sharing is a means to reduce these pressures without making nonstandard employment a precarious source of livelihood (as the zero-hours contracts currently are). It is essential that sources of income are secure and, most importantly, not contingent on past or present labor-market participation. Thus, neither the eligibility for social insurance nor its amount should be sourced from the employment contract, as in the Bismarckian welfare state, because this discourages labor-market exit. Rather, it should be based on national citizenship or, even better, denizenship, emulating the Scandinavian form of welfare provision.

The main value of this model lies in securing every citizen a place in the productive economy yet decoupling sources of livelihood from one's entrapment in the process of economic production. Left-leaning critics of "flexicurity" (flexible and secure employment) would typically argue against labor-market activation (i.e., retraining of the unemployed) and in favor of generous welfare provision.[12] They would also embrace the "defamilialized" welfare regime for its active public policy allowing full participation of men and women in the labor market. From this perspective, social justice becomes a matter of balancing labor-market deregulation and liberalization with high levels of social security spending, itself sourced from taxing the productive economic actors, including the technology that is replacing human labor.[13]

However, perceiving social justice predominantly as a matter of maintaining high social security spending implies a "productivist" normative conception of social justice: that is, understanding it in the narrow terms of *production* and *redistribution* of wealth. I have charted, however, a different normative perspective— nondomination as emancipation from the accelerating productivist imperatives of capitalism. From this perspective, social justice is a matter of the fair distribution of the growing decom-modification potential of advanced industrial democracies.[14] In this sense, voluntary employment flexibility charts a normative territory on which equality and freedom can be reconciled as "real freedom to make choices." Both entry into and exit from the labor market, due to their voluntary nature, contribute to social inclusion. This criterion is a form of egalitarianism applied to autonomy but, importantly, this is a socially embedded auton-omy that credits both productive activity and freedom from gainful employment as valuable sources of selfhood and tools of social integration. Indeed, community is not constructed by work, whether paid or not, as James Chamberlain has argued in a compelling way in his *Undoing Work, Rethinking Community* (2018). However, even if productive activity does not have a con-stitutive function for human communities, it could be a means of social integration, as it is a tool of generating the resources for satisfying material and ideational needs. The task, therefore, is to minimize reliance on paid employment both for a person's socialization and for the satisfaction of needs.

Societies that combine a limited yet secure employment within a liberalized labor market with citizenship-based, rather than employment-based social provision maximize both access to sources of income and the possibility for labor-market exit (decommodification). Such a combination would ensure the maximization of earning *opportunity* (though not necessarily *levels* of income) without denigrating labor-market exit. This would, in turn, enable voluntary reduction of the time spent in gainful employment and engagement with creative work and lei-sure. Mainstreaming voluntary part-time work is a form of pol-icy design of labor markets that exemplifies this model of social justice.

Within the European Union, such a combination of flexible employment and social provision based on EU denizenship would be the basis for redesigning the European Social Model to focus on fighting insecurity rather than exclusively on countering inequality (a typical priority for the Left) or improving working conditions (a typical commitment of the political Right). The question then emerges of how social provision would be funded.

As robust social transfers (from "rich" to "poor" member states) at this point seem to be out of the question, a trans-European system of social provision cannot be funded via substantial national contributions.[15] Instead, it could be supported via a proper European Sovereign Wealth Fund—an independent source of revenue operating on market principles. The fund could be sourced by socializing the rent exploited by companies not properly exposed to competition (including banks) via, for instance, increased taxation or by placing these companies in public hands, along the lines of a trans-European rail system publicly owned but operated on market principles of cost and revenue management. The funds for social provision would be managed through a European Social Stability Mechanism akin to the current Financial Stability Mechanism and under rules of democratic accountability, thereby allowing democratic publics to have a say on the allocation of productive inputs and social surplus.

A political economy of trust with its two components (regarding domestic economies and the global market) will remedy the discrepancy between the public absorption of risk and the private accumulation of gains that afflicts our societies. It will increase the space for creativity by decreasing competition, and it will enable the satisfaction of human needs without inflating these needs. As the combined effect of these measures is to constrain the competitive production of profit, it would strike at the very constitutive dynamic of capitalism. Implementing them would have an immanent transformative effect. At the same time, by generating personal stability and liberating time from productivist commitments and pressures, the measures would also supply the material conditions for an imaginative and constructive political mobilization for overcoming capitalism. Indeed, we do not need a terminal crisis of capitalism, a revolutionary project, or a grand utopia to make this happen.

CONCLUSION

The Radical Pragmatism of Bidding
Capitalism Farewell

*If we appear to seek the unattainable, then let it be known that
we do so to avoid the unimaginable.*

—The Port Huron Statement of Students for a Democratic Society (1962)

For over two centuries now, at least since the publication of Adam Smith's *The Wealth of Nations* in 1776, capitalism has drawn accolades for being, purportedly, the engine not only of material prosperity, but also of scientific innovation (never mind Galileo, Newton, and Leibniz), the maximization of freedoms, and therefore of overall individual and societal well-being. The alternatives that have been tried went terribly wrong.

The noncapitalist dictatorships that proliferated throughout the twentieth century often appropriated the label "communism" in an effort to justify themselves. However, they ended up putting in place a social system that shared capitalism's greatest malignities. As the Czech dissident philosopher Václav Havel observed, these two sociopolitical systems are incarnations of the same exploitative, alienating logic. Under state socialism, as under capitalism, he noted, people are afflicted by a condition he called *samopohyb*, which translates as "self-waste." This malaise is incurred by our submission to "the irrational momentum of anonymous, impersonal, and inhuman power—the power of ideologies, systems, apparatus, bureaucracy, artificial languages, and political slogans" (Havel [1984] 1991, 269).[1]

Whatever capitalism's progressive role might have been (within the dynamics of the "creative destruction" Karl Marx discerned and Joseph Schumpeter made famous), it seems that its penchant for destruction has come to trump its creative powers. As already discussed, that evidence transcends the financial, economic, and social crises that will be known as the Great Recession of the early twenty-first century. This recession brought about not a crisis *of* capitalism but a crisis *for* capitalism— roadblocks on the path of the competitive production of profit that capitalism is already finding ways to overcome, above all by increasing competitive pressures and spreading them throughout society. At the nadir of the economic slowdown, calls were voiced for overthrowing capitalism (from the Left), for stabilizing it (from the Right), or for reforming it to make it more inclusive (from the political center). In this book, I have suggested that there is a fourth option: overcoming capitalism by subverting it from within. This can be done through radical practices that strike at the very constitutive dynamic of capitalism, namely the competitive production of profit.

We live in a rather peculiar moment in the life of capitalism that is ripe with transformative tendencies. These do not, of course, all push in the same direction. On the one hand, they converge into a condition I described as a "crisis of the crisis of capitalism": we are stuck in a mode of perpetual crisis management that has become the new normal, with societies in a state of chronic inflammation. On the other hand, that very condition contains an emancipatory potential.

My investigation into the transformative potential of our times unfolded as a particular form of analysis: an internal (immanent) critique of lived experiences of injustice originating from the key contradictions of contemporary capitalism. The transformative pressures that had already beset advanced industrial democracies at the close of the last century—in particular those generated by the new economy of open borders and technological upheaval—have been my main focus. The economic meltdown of 2007–2008 and the decade-long recession that followed enabled ruling elites to consolidate a transition that had already begun in the early twenty-first century. They reinvented neoliberal capitalism as a yet more virulent form that I named "precarity capitalism." This new modality inherits many of the features of its predecessors. From its neoliberal dad, it adopts the desire to build competitiveness at any social cost. From its nanny—the "welfare state"—it borrows rusted redistributive tools and adjusts them to the frantic pursuit of competitiveness. Public authority in this new format of capitalism actively allocates opportunities to individual economic actors by helping them enhance their pre-existing advantage in the global economy. At the same time, it transfers risks to society or to weaker economic actors through a policy approach I named "socially irresponsible rule." I chose this formulation not in order to add yet another pejorative term to the portrayals of contemporary capitalism, but to stress the logic of policy action that aims at and often achieves economic efficiency, but does so without regard for the impact on society.

I observed that, paradoxically, despite the devastation this has brought to our societies (such as growing precarity and environmental destruction), no legitimacy crisis of democratic capitalism has ensued. This enduring stability is displayed by the diminished electoral support for Left parties and movements, the growing support to economically liberal elites (the center-right keeps winning elections), and the rise of populist movements that defend national capitalism against "foreign" capitalism. There is no liberating utopia emerging from the clash between defenders of "our" capitalism and the adepts of global capitalism. Fighting for its political survival, the radical Left has neither the credentials nor the social support to call for a revolution.

This is the case, I argued, because of the negative dynamics of politicization that emerge in a context of massive economic, social, and physical uncertainty. Fear triggers conservative, often reactionary, instincts. The road to imaginative, forward-looking politics seems firmly blocked. Without a guiding utopia, without a revolution in the offing, and without a terminal crisis of capitalism, we seem to be stuck in the darkest historical form of capitalism so far—one of merciless competition for profit that is wrecking our everyday lives, corroding our democracies, and devastating our natural environment.

However, I have discerned an emancipatory potential elsewhere, rooted in the two main contradictions of contemporary capitalism, which I discussed as "surplus employability" and "acute job dependency." The former arises in the tension between, on the one hand, the unprecedented technological capacity of our societies to produce material prosperity with minimum input of human labor (i.e., what I described as the significant *decommodification potential* of our societies) and, on the other, ever-growing pressures to remain employed and employable (i.e., increased *commodification pressures*). The second contradiction is the one between the growing reliance on employment as one's source of livelihood and the decreasing capacity of the political economy to supply the necessary jobs. Both contradictions are generated by the constitutive dynamic of capitalism: the competitive production of profit. As we have seen, in combination, these two antinomies of contemporary capitalism have entailed the intensification of competition, which in turn has led to an unprecedented spread of economic uncertainty. Precarity is the social question of our time. That is why I named our current system "precarity capitalism." The vast variety of grievances (from impoverishment to poor mental health and wrecked family lives) has put capitalism on edge. They could cumulate and culminate in pressures for a radical transformation.

The difficulty is this: It is the political economy of uncertainty, of massive precariousness, that has been generating a widespread dissatisfaction with capitalism. And yet, that same uncertainty is fostering a conservative-to-reactionary political expression (politicization) of grievances, from "Save capitalism!" to "Close the borders!" That is why I suggested that reforms for countering social and economic uncertainty would provide the material conditions for reframing (politicizing) protest in a more radical and constructive direction, thereby enabling the angry multitude to become a political agent with a positive agenda.

Taxing the rich might not be a bad place to start. As to whether this would amount to saving capitalism or helping it dig its grave, the answer is: it can do both. Saving capitalism in the particular conjuncture of the early twenty-first century is, paradoxically, a condition for its overcoming. This is the case because rebooting the economic engine of capitalism by stabilizing production, employment, and income, as I have suggested, also creates the conditions for emancipatory political agency. Economic precariousness, just like poverty, has debilitating personal, political, and social effects. The massive economic and social uncertainty that marks the latest phase of capitalism has engendered such radical disempowerment that building capitalism with a human face—Robert Reich's (2015) "capitalism for the many, not the few"—is a much-needed emergency measure if we are ever to get a grip on our collective destiny. Urgent action is necessary for society to regain the steering wheel. We are therefore in need of what I called a "political economy of trust," one that ensures that everyone has a secure livelihood. I adumbrated some policy ideas that target economic insecurity, rather than inequality (the standard agenda of the political Left) or competitiveness (the agenda of the political Right). Without countering precarity, the spirit of enterprise and experimentation, be it artistic, economic, or political, cannot thrive. Bidding capitalism farewell would first demand that it fare well economically.

Yet, as we undertake to fight poverty and inequality, create stable and good jobs, and tend to other social emergencies of our times, we risk falling into the trap of what I described as the *paradox of emancipation*: namely, when we seek inclusion and equality within a model of well-being, we inadvertently endorse that model together with the injustices, beyond inequality and exclusion, it continues to generate, from damaging the natural environment to subordinating human existence to the pressures of production and consumption (Havel's "self-waste"). From where would the social energies come to make the step from stabilization of capitalism to emancipation from it, from saving capitalism to overcoming it?

Since its inception in the eighteenth century, capitalism has created opponents among groups to whom the long-term benefits of the market system are less apparent—typically workers, even though, as Schumpeter reminds us, "the labor movement is not essentially socialist, just as socialism is not necessarily laborite or proletarian" and socialism "would be nowhere without the intellectual leader of bourgeois extraction" (1943, 310–11). Indeed, opposition to capitalism has brewed on the basis of the unequal distribution of life-chances. It was first opposed by the aristocracy, whose social status it threatened, and later by the impoverished working classes. In other words, the groups opposing capitalism have been those located on the losing side in the distribution of power (victims of what I described as "relational domination"), as well as those who were on the losing side in terms of ownership of productive capital (victims of "structural domination").

Marx and most of his contemporaries asserted that a tendency toward socialism was latent in capitalism and held that the laboring class was the historical protagonist to enact this tendency. For them, emancipation in the form of socialism meant primarily liberation of labor from exploitation. This has been the predominant position of the Left in the course of the twentieth century. The context of the early twenty-first century offers a radical alternative of a different nature. The current emancipatory opening combines three components regarding the *nature* of discontent, the *agent* of change, and the *mechanisms* of change. Let me say a few words on each, summing up the arguments of the book.

We stand at a tipping point in history when acute dissatisfaction with capitalism is rising, not on account of its poor economic performance or the unfair distribution of wealth, but rather its excellent economic performance, its intensity. In other words, as the real income and the social clout of the working class has risen, exploitation is no longer the key engine of social injustice. Instead, it is the competitive production of profit—the key dynamic of capitalism—that is felt as harmful by all participants in this process. It is for the first time that acute injustices are experienced from, and social hostility is directed at, both the competitive and the productivist components in the operation of capitalism. What is being challenged is not simply the unfair distribution of wealth, but, importantly, the very process through which wealth is generated and the impact this has on individuals, communities, and nature. This is the case because the trouble with current-day capitalism is not just material inequality, but a massive economic and social uncertainty afflicting a growing multitude of groups beyond the poor and the excluded. The intensified competitive pressures of globally integrated capitalism have also done tangible damage to the *winners* in the distribution of power—labor market insiders with good and well-paid jobs, owners and managers of capital—and is triggering their discontent.

This novel multifaceted discontent is shaping a powerful political force. A variety of interests across class divides, educational levels, and cultural identities are making diverse individuals converge into a multitude united by an overarching grievance against the impact the competitive production of profit is having on their lives as well as their social and natural environment. Mobilized in a mundane and inglorious anticapitalist revolution, these forces can perform a social change yet more radical than any proletarian class struggle could ever achieve.

Progressive politics since the birth of capitalism have proceeded in one of two ways. Both Social Democracy and Christian Democracy have sought to humanize capitalism through reforms such as redistribution of wealth. The radical Left has sought to overthrow it by a revolutionary expropriation of privately held productive assets and placing them in public hands. As I have argued, none of these measures are a threat to capitalism, because they do not hamper its constitutive dynamic— the competitive production of profit. It is worth recalling that the clash between the communist dictatorships and capitalist democracies during the Cold War perpetuated the competitive production of profit, which was simply pursued with different means.

However, the by now well-oiled political machinery of liberal democracy, despite the well-deserved criticism of its failings, is nevertheless able to deliver radical change through incremental policy responses to public preferences, as long as diverse publics push in the same direction. This logic of building influential alliances brought about the codification of basic rights (well before the advent of mass democracy), racial and gender equality (despite the opposition of numerical majorities and powerful minorities), as well as the post-WWII welfare state.

Symptomatic of the tangible potential of an anticapitalist shift in public opinion is that the idea of democratic socialism is gaining political influence in the United States, the flagship capitalist democracy. This was displayed by young Americans' enthusiastic support for Bernie Sanders in the run-up to the 2016 presidential elections. Membership in the Democratic Socialists of America increased tenfold between 2016 and 2018. The defeat of long-time Democratic boss and congressman Joe Crowley (a typical Democratic Party member of the neoliberal policy establishment) by democratic socialist Alexandria Ocasio-Cortez in the primaries in Queens, New York, in June 2018 has become emblematic of the phenomenon of "Socialist Millennials." Importantly, politically engaged millennials are mobilizing both against poverty and for saving the environment, concerns that rank as essentials of life. These two objectives can be achieved only through radical practices that go against the competitive production of profit—ergo, against capitalism—even if not all espouse the ideas of socialism or communism. Symptomatic of an emergent anticapitalist impetus is also the mainstreaming of concerns with inequality in the political discourse of all political families, after the "Occupy" movement broke a decades-long taboo over the mention of inequality in political discourse.

Exactly which political force is initiating these emancipatory policies is of lesser importance. For example, the European Pillar of Social Rights that was inaugurated in 2016 was an initiative of the center-right. In the United States, many of the job-protection policies President Trump has advocated or launched (such as pulling the country out of the Trans-Pacific Partnership) go against the competitive production of profit and have been endorsed by Left political groups as well.

These developments, just like the shock of angry Americans propelling a maverick presidential candidate through the democratic vote or the counterwave of political protest that accompanies Trump's presidency, signal that the technocratic politics of no alternatives (the TINA policy logic) that had paralyzed Western democracies for the previous three decades is over. The institutional channels of liberal democracies have been unblocked. They are effectively processing social discontent and translating it into pressures for radical alternatives. The grievances of the multitude against the effects of competitive profit production could thus obtain political expression through the mechanisms of democratic politics. This would amount to overcoming capitalism in the manner of what Antonio Gramsci called "passive revolution"—a significant, yet gradual metamorphosis of the social order, a radical but not rapturous change. Herein lies the radical nature of the current conjuncture, even as capitalism has recovered from the latest economic downturn, talk about crisis of capitalism has vanished, an organized revolutionary force is not in sight, and the utopian models for a postcapitalist society have largely been discarded.

There is yet another source of hope. The generation that is now coming of age—politically, culturally, economically—is wary of the dogmas of both capitalism and socialism and will not be captive to stale political prescriptions. The current context is not unlike that of half a century ago, when young people in the spring of 1968 turned their frustrations with the oppressive certitudes of the older generation into an upheaval of the political imagination that reached beyond the timid ambitions of inclusion and equality—they demanded a brand-new world. The year 1968 is behind us and offers no welcome blueprints. Yet a new multitude, more powerful in number and more bitter in its quiet discontent, is demanding a type of life that contemporary capitalism cannot deliver. We do not need the crutches of a utopia, a crisis, or a revolution to find the exit.

Appendix

SUMMARY OF THEORETICAL FRAMEWORK

I. ON SOCIAL ORGANIZATION

The **social order** of contemporary Western societies comprises **capitalism** as a system of social relations and **liberal democracy** as a system of political rule. Thus, capitalism can be combined with a variety of political systems (e.g., the democratic capitalism of the United States and Europe; China's autocratic capitalism). As a historically particular, modern social formation, capitalism is not to be reduced to "market economy" or "market society."

The **repertoire of capitalism** is a unity of the following core elements:

1. Two *systemic dynamics* (dynamics pertaining to the social system):

   (a) A *constitutive dynamic* (*operative logic*): the *competitive production of profit*. This combines three organizing principles: competition, profit-making, and production (the productivist, rather than creative, nature of work—i.e., labor engaged in the production of commodities). The constitutive dynamic shapes notions of life-chances (for a successful life and an accomplished self), before these chances are distributed.

(b) An enabling dynamic of *primitive appropriation*: the appropriation of what is to be deployed in the competitive pursuit of profit.

2. *Internal structure*: institutions with structuring effect that enact the constitutive dynamic, such as private property, management of the means of production, and the "free" labor contract. These institutions configure the social relations and shape the distribution of life-chances in society.

3. *Ethos*: worldviews orienting behavior and giving it the meaning of rational enterprise under individual initiative. These enable capitalism to source its *legitimacy* from the correlation between entrepreneurial risks and opportunities in the distribution of life-chances in society (see also *legitimation matrix*).

Modalities of capitalism are historical configurations of the repertoire of capitalism. Changes occur when new circumstances create new social opportunities and risks, when the correlation between risks and opportunities is disturbed, or when new public perceptions emerge about the fair distribution of life-chances. There are four such sequential modalities:

- liberal capitalism (nineteenth century);
- welfare capitalism (most of the twentieth century);
- neoliberal capitalism (late twentieth century); and
- precarity capitalism (early twenty-first century—current era).

Precarity capitalism is the latest historical articulation of the repertoire of capitalism. Its core features are: (1) generalization of precarity across social class, professional occupations, and income levels; (2) active redistribution of resources from weak economic actors to powerful ones by public authority in pursuit of global economic competitiveness; (3) fear-based motivation to engage in the system. This modality of capitalism is marked by two internal contradictions: *surplus employability* (the simultaneous increase of the decommodification potential of modern societies and the increase of commodification pressures) and *acute job dependency* (the tension between decreased availability of good jobs and increased reliance on a job as a source of livelihood).

Liberal democracy is a political system: that is, an institutionalized system of political rule. Its "repertoire" consists of:

1. *Operative logic/principle*: the competitive pursuit of public office;
2. *Structures* (institutions with structuring effect) enacting the operative logic, such as popular suffrage and competitive elections, constitutionally codified basic rights, and accountable government; and
3. *Ethos*: popular sovereignty understood as a rational enterprise of collective self-determination. This enables democracy to source its legitimacy from the values of individual autonomy and equality of citizenship (see also *legitimation matrix*).

Socialism is a system of social relations based on full socialization of the means of production, which are held either as communal property or by the central public authority.

II. ON LEGITIMACY

I deploy four concepts to discuss legitimation as a process in which the subjects of a given social order endorse it as being just:

ethos, legitimation matrix, framework of political reference, and *legitimacy deal*.

Ethos is the unity of cognitive and normative orientations regarding views about truth, appropriateness, and acceptability. It is the societal "common sense" or rationality.

The **legitimation matrix** is the set of normative resources from which the legitimacy of the social order is sourced—its ground rules of fairness. The legitimation matrix of a social order is composed of a set of broadly shared views about life-chances and their fair distribution. Since its inception, capitalism as a system of social relations has relied on the following ground rule: in an (idealized) market society, risks and opportunities are to be correlated for every participant. The legitimation matrix of liberal democracy as a political system stipulates the mutual accommodation between individual autonomy and collective self-determination. This arrangement is secured through another ground rule: equal citizenship. The legitimation matrix of democratic capitalism (a social order with capitalism as a social system and democracy as a political system) combines the rules that opportunities and risks be correlated and that all members have a say over the way life-chances are distributed. The legitimation matrix is the repository for the process of the *politicization* of social grievances into demands for policy action addressed to public authority.

The **framework of political reference** is a broader societal understanding (political common sense) regarding what counts as a politically relevant social concern (e.g., poverty, inequality, crime, environmental degradation). The *legitimacy deal* is located within this framework.

The **legitimacy deal** is the explicit legitimacy relationship between public authority and citizens. Located within the framework of political reference, it specifies which actions public authority is to perform for society in order to secure the fair distribution of life chances (political deliverables), as understood within the legitimation matrix. The legitimacy deal alters when the legitimation matrix is threatened, in order to safeguard it. This enables considerable changes within a given social system (engenders modalities of the system) in order to keeps it intact.

The four concepts are linked to each other in a descending range of validity and ascending range of specificity. That is, *ethos* has the largest scope of operation and is the least specific notion, while the *legitimacy deal* has the narrowest scope of validity and is the most specific notion among the four. They all enable the politicization of a social phenomenon into an object of policymaking.

Politicization is the process in the course of which a social phenomenon gains public notice and eventually becomes a salient object of policy.

The **right to politics** is the right to have a grievance of injustice be considered a relevant social concern and a valid object of policymaking. It secures an ongoing process of politicization via a continuous contestation of society's binding rules and practices. The spectrum of practices through which a grievance gains political relevance spans from deliberation to insurrection. The right to politics, together with the "right to have rights" (Arendt) and the "right to justification" (Forst) constitute a distinct category I call *meta-rights*; these are constitutive of the political, while ordinary rights (including the fundamental rights to life and liberty) determine the quality of the political (i.e., render political membership more rigorous).

A **crisis-of-crisis** is a condition of being stuck in a crisis. There are, in principle, three solutions to a crisis: death, returning to the precrisis situation, or transitioning to a new state. The perpetuation of crisis management into a new normal creates a situation

Table A.1 Summary of Key Concepts in the Analysis of Legitimacy

Term	Definition	Applied to capitalism as a social system	Applied to liberal democracy as a political system
Ethos	Behavior-orienting worldviews	Rational enterprise under individual initiative	Popular sovereignty as a rational enterprise of collective self-determination
Operative logic/ principle	The system's constitutive dynamic	Competitive profit production	Competitive pursuit of public office
Framework of political reference	Politically salient social concerns	Alters, constrained by the operative logic and oriented by the ethos	Alters, constrained by the operative logic and oriented by the ethos
Legitimation matrix	A set of ground rules that emerge as shared views regarding (1) what constitutes a life-chance and (2) the fair distribution of life-chances in society	Correlation between risks and opportunities in the distribution of life-chances	Individual autonomy and equality of citizenship within collective self-determination
Legitimacy deal	The relationship between public authority and citizens: the legitimate and legitimacy-conferring functions of public authority (political deliverables)	Regards the overall institutionalized social order and alters according to the particular politicization of social phenomena	Regards the overall institutionalized social order and alters according to the particular politicization of social phenomena

in which the crisis itself enters a crisis (crisis of the crisis): the crisis is not resolved and none of the usual three outcomes applies. Precarity becomes a perpetual feature of life, embracing all social strata.

III. ON DOMINATION

The systemic dynamics, structures, and distributive outcomes of the operation of capitalism entail three types of domination and their attendant forms of injustice:

1. **Relational domination** consists in the subordination of one group of actors to another by force of the unequal distribution of power in society. Corresponding forms of injustice (*relational injustice*) are inequality and exclusion. Typical remedies are inclusion and equalization of power (via, e.g., expanding the electoral franchise or the redistribution of wealth). Not all inequalities engender relational domination.

2. **Systemic domination** consists in the subjugation of all members of society to the operative logic of the social system, including the winners in the asymmetrical distribution of power. In capitalism, it is engendered by the imperative of competitive production of profit to which the owners and managers of capital, as well as workers, succumb. *Systemic injustice* has to do with social harm beyond the unequal distribution of social advantage and disadvantage; this is harm engendered by the very notion of what constitutes a social advantage (ideal of a successful life and notion of accomplished self) issued by the operative logic of the system, that is, the system-specific definition of social status. Thus, labor commodification (treating a person's capacity to work as a good produced for market exchange) and alienation afflict

all who are engaged in the process of competitive profit production, while the destruction of the environment is a harm suffered by the whole of humanity, be it in different degrees. Emancipation from systemic domination would necessitate the eradication of the operative logic of the system—in the case of capitalism, the competitive production of profit.

3. **Structural domination** concerns the constraints on judgment and action that the main structuring institutions of the social system impose on actors. *Structural injustice* consists in the incapacity of some actors to control the institutions through which the operative logic of the social system is enacted, which translates as their impotency to affect the "rules of the game." A typical example in the case of capitalism is the exploitation of labor, which cannot be remedied via redistribution or higher salaries. This is the case because the competitive production of profit necessitates that some of the surplus value produced by the workers be reinvested in maintaining the competitiveness of the company that employs them. Emancipation from structural injustice necessitates the abolishment of the institutions engendering structural domination. In the case of capitalism, these are the private property of productive assets and the market as a mechanism for the allocation of productive inputs and surplus (but not as a mechanism for meeting supply and demand in the distribution of goods for personal consumption).

The **paradox of emancipation** is a situation in which success in fighting one form of domination comes at the price of aggravating another form. Struggles against inequality and exclusion (relational domination) tend to enhance the value of the social system within which inequality and exclusion are being sought, thus increasing the legitimacy of an unjust system.

Table A.2 Summary of Types of Domination and Forms of Injustice

Type of domination	Types of injustice	Remedy
Relational: the subordination of one group of actors to another by force of unequal distribution of power	Inequality and exclusion	Equalization of resources and inclusion
Structural: the constraints on judgment and action the main social institutions impose on actors	Incapacity of actors to control the structures that direct the distribution of life-chances	Abolishing the social institutions that engender structural domination
Systemic: the subordination of all members of society to the operative logic of the social system	Harm incurred by the system-specific definition of social status	Eradication of the system's operative logic

Emancipatory practice is an enduring pattern of activities (social interactions) that aim at the elimination of systemic, structural, and relational domination.

Radical or **revolutionary practice** is emancipatory practice aiming to eradicate systemic domination.

NOTES

INTRODUCTION: "HOW COME?" ASKED THE BEFUDDLED LEFT

1. So did economist Joseph Stiglitz (2003) describe the twentieth century's last decade, as spectacular job creation, technological innovation that spurred productivity growth, and low inflation all combined to secure unprecedented prosperity in the West and elsewhere, before he laid bare its clay foundation.

2. The European United Left/Nordic Green Left group of the European Parliament commissioned me to make the study in 2002 in view of the upcoming 2004 European elections. A version of the report I submitted in 2003 was published in Azmanova (2004).

3. Reportedly, even Marx refused to identify himself as a Marxist, that is, a thinker subscribing to a method of socioeconomic analysis based on abstract laws, derived from Marx's historical account of nineteenth-century European capitalism (Engels, "Letter to Bernstein," 1882; Engels, "Letter to Schmidt," 1890).

4. Gloria Steinem is famous for her frustration with the obscurity of feminist scholarship rooted in Derridean deconstruction. The renowned feminist has often jokingly threatened to put a "Beware! Deconstruction Ahead!" sign on the road to Harvard and Yale (see Steinem 2015).

1. THE CRISIS OF CAPITALISM, ALMOST

1. For both thinkers, crises are a core feature of the dynamics of capitalism—a process in which the "gale of creative destruction" that

technological innovation fosters eliminates the old as it brings forth the new. Schumpeter appropriated the idea from Marx and popularized it.

2. See Blanchard (2010) for an elaborate claim that the crisis resulted from policies based on economic analysis bereft of the ethical considerations that political economist Adam Smith and religious thinker John Calvin (in their analyses of work, consumption, and trade) deemed essential for economic activity, namely honesty, "neighbor love," and respect for the law.

3. Adopted at its congress in Lisbon, December 7–8, 2018: https://www .pes.eu/export/sites/default/.galleries/Documents-gallery/Resolu tions_PES_Congress_2018.pdf_2063069299.pdf.

4. As economist Michael Roberts has noted (2016), the reason for the protracted postcrisis period of slow growth and weakened productivity is the fact that the profitability of capital is too low. He contends that rapid economic growth will not return until another slump restores a sufficiently elevated rate of profit, ensured by more austerity (cuts in public investment and wages) and constraints on the bargaining power of labor.

5. President Trump was elected on a platform against open markets (globalization) rather than against the free domestic market. The prospect of the far-right Marine Le Pen winning the 2017 French presidential elections mobilized electoral support to Emmanuel Macron, a former Socialist politician who publicly renounced socialism and endorsed the free market. As minister of economy, Macron had supervised the liberalization of the French economy. On assuming the presidency, he embarked on cutting corporate taxes and loosening France's wealth tax to exclude all financial assets, pledging to cut sixty billion euros in public spending within five years.

6. Reported by the Feeding America network at "What Is Food Insecurity?," https://www.feedingamerica.org/hunger-in-america/food-in security.

7. To look at the electoral landscape immediately after the crisis, elections in 2010 and 2011 brought to power the center-right in Spain, Portugal, Switzerland, Finland, Andorra, Ireland, Italy, Denmark, Britain, and the Netherlands—to consider only the "mature" democracies of Europe. In that period, the majority of the vote went to the center-left only in

Sweden, where the Social Democrats scored just 0.6 percentage points higher than the economically liberal Moderate Rally Party. (The vote for the former dropped significantly in the next round, and the vote for the latter increased considerably.)

2. CAPITALISM UNDER SCRUTINY: FROM CONCEPT TO CRITIQUE

1. This idea of a difference between *critical* and *traditional* theory that the first generation of Frankfurt School authors developed is akin to the vision Robert Cox later advanced (1981) about the difference between *critical* and *problem-solving* theory in laying out the foundation of a critical social theory within the British school of International Political Economy.

2. "The distinguishing feature of Communism is not the abolition of property generally, but the abolition of bourgeois property" and "We by no means intend to abolish the personal appropriation of the products of labour," writes Marx in *The Communist Manifesto* (1848), clarifying that when capital is converted into common property, "personal property is not thereby transformed into social property." What is changed is the social character of property—i.e., it loses its class character.

3. In Robert Cox's formulation, "critical theory allows for a normative choice in favour of a social and political order different from the prevailing order, but it limits the range of choice to alternative orders which are feasible transformations of the existing world" (Cox 1981, 130).

4. However, this grounding of the perspective of critique within the self-understandings of the society that is being analyzed should not imply that this self-understanding cannot be an object of criticism. As Adorno notes, "the alternatives—either calling culture as a whole into question from outside under the general concept of ideology, or confronting a culture with the norms that it has crystallized out of itself, cannot be recognized by critical theory. To insist on the choice between immanence and transcendence is a relapse into the traditional logic which was the object of Hegel's polemic against Kant" (Adorno 1970–1986, vol. 10, 25). For an extensive exposition of this perspective of critique, see Benhabib 1986 and Finlayson 2014.

5. "According to the materialist conception of history, the ultimately determinant element in history is the production and reproduction of real life. . . . Hence if somebody twists this into saying that the economic element is the only determining one, he transforms that proposition into a meaningless, abstract and senseless phrase." (Engels, "Letter to J. Bloch," Sept. 21, 1890, in Marx and Engels 1962, vol. 2, 488).

6. See Jaeggi (2017) for an elaborate articulation of the need to perceive the economy as social practice.

7. "Economic theory," observed Pierre Bourdieu, "has allowed to be foisted upon it a definition of the economy of practices which is the historical invention of capitalism; and by reducing the universe of exchanges to mercantile exchange, which is objectively and subjectively oriented toward the maximization of profit, i.e., (economically) *self-interested*, it has implicitly defined the other forms of exchange as noneconomic, and therefore *disinterested*" (Bourdieu 1986, 241).

8. This is a central point in the debates in Adorno et al. (1976).

9. Adorno makes this remark in "Something's Missing: A Conversation between Ernst Bloch and Theodor Adorno on the Contradictions of Utopian Longing" (Bloch 1988, 1– 17, 12).

10. Jia Tolentino's dissection of the white supremacist demonstrations in Charlottesville, Virginia,in the summer of 2017 provides a perfect example of using a perceived pathology as an entry point for critique. Such mobilizations might appear as an "aberrant travesty in a progressive enclave," yet they are a symptom that "much evil can be obscured by the appearance of good," i.e., by the purportedly progressive stance of upper-middle-class America (Tolentino 2017).

11. "Without the anticipation of that structural moment of the whole, which in individual observations can hardly ever be adequately realized, no individual observation would find its relative place" (Adorno 1976, 107). See also Jay 1984 for a detailed discussion of Adorno's ontology of the social as a fractured yet structured totality.

12. Joseph Schumpeter, whose understanding of capitalism is strongly informed by Marx, speaks of capitalism as a "civilization," "social order," and "social system" (1943). In his analysis, the economic system of capitalism (characterized by private initiative, production for a market, and credit) tends to threaten the institutional survival of the

capitalist civilization by "undermining the social positions on which the 'order' rests" (1928, 48).

13. In earlier work, I have referred to capitalism as an institutionalized social order (Azmanova 2012c, 2014), in line with analyses advanced by Wolfgang Streeck (2010) and Nancy Fraser (2014a, 2015). However, I prefer to use the term "social order" in referring to a larger sociopolitical entity such as democratic capitalism or capitalist democracies, within which capitalism is viewed as a particular system of social relations. The capitalist social system can be combined with a variety of political systems (e.g., the autocracies of contemporary China and Russia or the absolute monarchies of eighteenth-century Europe).

14. For the recent reengagement of critical theory of Frankfurt School origin with a critique of the political economy of capitalism (beyond redistributive injustices), see Hartmann and Honneth (2006), Fraser (2009, 2013, 2014a, 2014b), Azmanova (2010, 2011b, 2012c), and Honneth (2014), to mention just the works that initiated the turn. For more recent iterations, see Fraser and Jaeggi (2018) and the contributions in Deutscher and Lafont (2017).

15. This synchronic (in time) existence of a model of capitalism is discussed in the "varieties of capitalism" literature, generated by the pioneering work of Peter Hall and David Soskice. The variation typically extends from "liberal market economies" such as the United States and Britain to "coordinated market economies" such as Japan, Germany, and the northern European states, passing through the "mixed" type we find in southern European countries such as France, Italy, Spain, and Portugal. (See Hall and Soskise 2001.)

16. For a detailed analysis of the status of competition in Marx's account of capitalism, see Palermo 2017.

17. The textbook definition of the market as a mechanism of meeting supply and demand applies to a variety of social systems and is not a peculiarity of capitalism. The market as a mechanism of exchange of commodities (goods produced for the purpose of market exchange), including the labor market as a mechanism of commodification of labor, is a distinctive feature of capitalism. While the market as a mechanism of exchange of goods does secure the most efficient satisfaction of human needs (i.e., supply meeting demand), the market as a mechanism of commodity exchange first creates needs through ever-expanding

production and consumption, which it then satisfies. This point, first made by Marx, has been extensively developed by Herbert Marcuse (see Marcuse [1932] 1973, [1933] 1973, 1964). Nancy Fraser has offered a useful articulation (drawing on Marx) of the "distributive" and "allocative" functions of markets. Under many social formations, markets are a basic tool for distribution of goods for personal consumption. The *differentia specifica* of capitalist markets is that they are also used for the allocation of societal resources (inputs into production) as well as for the allocation of society's surplus (Fraser and Jaeggi 2018, 24–28). In this sense, I speak of markets as a primary mechanism of economic governance under capitalism.

18. Weber introduces the term "life-chance" to speak about "the probability of procuring goods, gaining a position in life, and finding inner satisfaction" ([1922] 1978, vol. 1, 302). It refers to a societal shared understanding of a successful life and an accomplished self, as well as to the individual psychological experiences of such an achievement.

19. Weber defines ethos in terms of ethical ideals having important formative influences on conduct. In this sense, he talks about the ethos or "economic spirit" of an economic system (Weber [1904–1905] 1992, 27).

20. This concerns "the state capacity to manage and distribute societal resources in ways that contribute to the achievement of prevailing notions of justice" (Offe 1985, 5).

21. I have previously called this hermeneutic level of shared meanings a *phronetic constitution* of public reason—a matrix within which issues are articulated as being relevant to the participants (and, thus, objects of judgment) despite disagreement on the content of norms. This prediscursive code makes the variety of conflicting claims comprehensible to the participants (Azmanova 2012b).

22. This account updates the taxonomy I developed in Azmanova 2018b and 2016a. In even earlier work, I distinguish only between relational and structural forms of domination (Azmanova 2012b, 2014). Steven Klein (2019 forthcoming) has developed a similar three-part typology of direct, structural, and abstract domination.

23. I am grateful to Steven Lukes for prompting me to make that clarification (private correspondence, February 24, 2018).

24. For the ways in which authors of the Frankfurt School tradition have addressed issues of systemic domination, see Azmanova 2014.

25. The former has been discussed by Hannah Arendt and Thomas Jefferson as the tendency for people to vote as (private) individuals rather than (public) citizens. The latter harm has been most eloquently addressed by Alexis de Tocqueville. Himself an adept of democracy, he nevertheless notes that democracies are marked by inherent instability of legislation and administration; they are susceptible to the whim of majorities and to the tyranny of public opinion; their "laws are almost always ineffective and inopportune" and "the men who are entrusted with the direction of public affairs . . . are frequently inferior, in both capacity and morality, . . . are unskilful and sometimes contemptible," while exercising arbitrary power "still greater than in despotic states. Ultimately . . . democracy, pushed to its furthest limits, is therefore prejudicial to the art of government, . . . the measures that it unwittingly adopts are frequently opposed to its own cause." (Tocqueville [1835] 1990, 1:209, 211–12, 238, 240–41, 263–71).

26. My take on domination generally dovetails with the recasting Moishe Postone (1993) has performed of Marx's analysis of capitalism to highlight an impersonal form of social domination generated by labor itself and not simply with market mechanisms and private property. However, the further articulation of three types of domination, as well as shifting attention from commodity production to competitive profit production, allows us to capture the difference between forms of suffering such as poverty whose remedy can be sought through redistribution and tools of political emancipation and forms that can be alleviated only by fighting the competitive profit production (e.g., environmental degradation, work-induced mental illness).

27. I am grateful to Maeve Cooke and Rainer Forst for prompting me to make this clarification.

3. IDEOLOGIES FOR THE NEW CENTURY

1. Reported in James Polity, "Migration Opens the Door to Italy's Populists," *Financial Times*, August 1, 2017, https://www.ft.com/content /b964453a-72b1–11e7-aca6-c6bdo7df1a3c.

2. Gordon Brown launched this slogan at Labour's annual conference in 2007; it was used largely in the anti-EU mobilization for the referendum in June 2016, when 51.9 percent voted for Britain to leave the European Union (Brexit).

3. The lecture was delivered at the "Philosophers Bridge the Bosphorus" seminars in Istanbul, May 19–24, 2010, http://www.resetdoc.org/story /00000021088.

4. In the 1990s, right-wing and/or protest parties gained considerable electoral support and even entered the legislatures of the mature democracies of Western Europe, Canada, and Australia, as well as the young postcommunist democracies of East and Central Europe (Azmanova 2004; Norris 2005).

5. The Freedom of Services Directive of the EU (Directive 2006/123/EC) made it possible for a worker from any member state (e.g., a Polish plumber) to work in any other state (e.g., France) under the former's labor laws. Thus, a plumber employed in France via a Polish company would be paid the Polish wages, which are much lower than French wages.

6. Tea Party members place little emphasis on the threat of immigrants taking American jobs; their major concern is the illegitimate use of government funds (through public assistance or use of government services) by unauthorized immigrants (Skocpol, Williamson, and Coggin 2011).

7. In the run-up to the French presidential elections in 2012, Front National general secretary Steeve Briois reproached Jean-Luc Mélanchon, the president of Front de Gauche, saying that his pro-immigrant positions made him an enemy of the working people, rather than "the French people," as would have been the case until recently. ("Mélenchon, par ses positions ouvertement immigrationnistes et anti-françaises, est l'ennemi du peuple ouvrier," quoted in "Le Front national pris en faux par Mélenchon," *Liberation*, May 30, 2012.)

8. See, for instance, Yalda Hakim, "Migrant Crisis: 'Hipster Right' Group Trying to Stop Rescue Ships," BBC News, July 8, 2017, http://www .bbc.com/news/world-europe-40505337.

9. The first modern phase of globalization, from the seventeenth to the late nineteenth century, was that of empires. For the historical stages and the various processes driving global interdependence, see Mann (1986–2012), Held (1999), and Held and McGrew (2007).

10. Surveys indicated that the issues motivating the rejection of the European Constitutional Treaty in France and the Netherlands in 2005, across the left–right divide, were fear of delocalization of jobs, fear of immigration, and excessive economic liberalization (European Commission 2005a, 2005b). The predominant association in public perception of the EU with open border policy (globalization and enlargement) explains the radical drop in support for EU integration among French Socialists: as compared to the vote on the Maastricht Treaty in 1992, support for the EU has fallen sharply among Socialist and Green voters, who previously supported both European integration and enlargement.

11. We might recall the Enron financial scandal of 2000, the Angolagate (arms-for-oil) scandal in France, the conviction of former French president Jacques Chirac for abuse of public funds during his election campaign in the 1990s, the Augusta affair in Belgium in the 1980s (aviation firms bribing officeholders), or the 2009 Parliamentary expenses scandal in the UK, to mention just a few of the developments that undermined public trust in political and economic elites well before the social effects of the financial crisis were felt.

12. In an EU-15 country sample, the decrease of trust in political institutions is highest in countries where austerity is a result of governments bailing out banks with public money (Roth, Nowak-Lehmann, and Otter, 2011).

13. I am grateful to Claus Offe for helping me articulate this point, which I address more extensively in Azmanova 2004.

14. How much decisional power to leave to King Louis XVI was the most divisive issue among the deputies of the French National Constituent Assembly, who gathered in the summer of 1789 to produce the nation's first written constitution. (It was adopted in 1791.) The antiroyalist revolutionaries seated themselves to the left of the presiding officer, while the supporters of the monarchy gathered to his right. Worth noting is that the Monarchiens ("Monarchists"), also called Democratic Royalists, were advocating a model similar to the British one (a constitutional monarchy with a two-chamber parliament): that is, both sides sought legitimacy in democratic values.

15. As the competition for votes targets citizens' final choice, alternatives are best presented as binary oppositions along a left-right dimension. An additional factor for the unidimensional structure of choice,

especially in multiparty systems, is the need for coalition formation. The building of political alliances to form governments makes it necessary that ideological divergence along some lines be ignored. (Within the ample body of literature on this, see, for instance: Schattschneider 1948; Sartori 1976; Oppenhuis 1995; Fuchs and Klingemann 1990; Thomassen 1994.)

16. The labels used in the figures correspond to European politics. The logic of aggregation of public preferences is the same in the United States, with the Democratic Party occupying the top left quadrant and the Republican Party the bottom right one.

17. Ronald Inglehart has been tracing this trend since the 1970s via the World Values Survey (http://www.worldvaluessurvey.org/wvs.jsp). In his account, the postindustrial revolution brought about the transition from the "old politics" of bread-and-butter concerns such as income and housing to "new politics" centered on lifestyle, self-expression, citizen democracy, identity rights, and concerns with the environment; this eventually engendered a new political culture (Inglehart 1977, 2008). See also the contributions in Clark and Hoffman-Martinot (1998).

18. As Peter Mair has put it, in a context of increased social mobility and heterogeneity, "meanings are no longer shared and the implications of political stances on the left or on the right become almost unreadable" (Mair 2007b, 24).

19. The 2004 European elections gave the parliamentary group of the European Liberal Democrats by far the highest increase in electoral gains. This group preserved its improved position at the June 2009 elections. This phenomenon was replicated on the level of national elections across Europe. (See Azmanova 2011a for further details.)

20. Pelosi made this remark in a CNN "town hall" interview in January 2017, when asked by Trevor Hill whether the Democratic Party could move further left on economic issues, quoting evidence that the majority of young adults in the United States reject capitalism. CNN, "Pelosi: Democrats Are Capitalists," http://www.cnn.com/videos /politics/2017/02/01/nancy-pelosi-town-hall-capitalism-sot.cnn.

21. As argued by Bernard Cassen, founder of the French protest party *Attac* (quoted in Harman 2007).

22. The notion of "free markets" denotes a minimal regulation of a domestic market, a laissez-faire capitalism. By contrast, market openness

concerns the rules governing exchanges between domestic economies, usually through trade and investment. One could conceive of exchanges between highly regulated domestic economies (nonfree but open markets), closed domestic free market economies (autarchies), and mutually integrated free domestic markets (open free markets).

23. "Ni patrie, ni patron. Ni Le Pen, ni Macron. On vaut mieux que ça" ("Neither the Fatherland nor the Boss. Neither le Pen nor Macron. We deserve better"). Under these slogans, high-school students across France walked in what the media named "a savage march" before the final round of the French presidential elections in April 2017.

4. THE LIFE AND TIMES OF
DEMOCRATIC CAPITALISM

1. I refer here to *social* risks and opportunities, ones entailed by the particular organization of the system of social relations. The unequal distribution of risks and opportunities among citizens that is due to random distribution does not qualify as social risks and opportunities. I am thankful to Philippe Schmitter for prompting me to make this clarification. This aligns with my conceptualization of injustice as social injustice, even as I agree with Judith Shklar's (1992) position that one cannot set rigid rules to distinguish instances of misfortune from injustice.

2. Tocqueville makes this point repeatedly in the two volumes of *Democracy in America*. Let me just quote this: "I think that democratic communities have a natural taste for freedom . . . But for equality their passion is ardent, insatiable, incessant, invincible; they call for equality in freedom; and if they cannot obtain that, they still call for equality in slavery. They will endure poverty, servitude, barbarism, but they will not endure aristocracy" (Tocqueville [1835] 1990, 2:97).

3. In the United States, President Franklin Delano Roosevelt spoke of the need for a "great cooperative movement" to cope with "national emergency productive of widespread unemployment and disorganization of industry" (Speech of June 16, 1933, on the National Industrial Recovery Act, http://www.presidency.ucsb.edu/ws/?pid=14673).

4. The first taxonomy captures variation in the degree to which the political economy is coordinated. Here, variation typically extends from "liberal market economies" to "coordinated market economies" (Hall

and Soskise 2001). The second taxonomy, introduced by Gøsta Esping-Andersen (1990), captures variation in the nature and generosity of social benefits provision. Within it, national varieties are clustered into "liberal," "conservative," and "social-democratic" types of welfare regimes.

5. The term "corporatism" refers not to business corporations but to organized economic interests such as guilds, trade unions, and employer organizations, whose influence in the economy marginalized the small enterprise based on individual initiative and competitiveness that had been the key player under liberal capitalism.

6. For an overview of the various hypotheses about the drivers of this change (as well as the most compelling explanation), see Reich 2007, 50–87.

7. By "neoliberalism," I refer to the return to socially disembedded markets in the late twentieth century that came to be commonly called "neoliberal capitalism," a political project that originated in the late 1960s but was fully implemented only in the 1980s. See Harvey 2005. The term "neoliberalism" emerged earlier with quite a different connotation, with reference to social market economy administered by the welfare state (what I here discuss as "welfare capitalism"). Alexandre Rüstow coined it in 1938 to refer to a doctrine (known also as *ordoliberalism*) marked by state intervention in the economy to secure growth and market efficiency. In his "Neo-Liberalism and Its Prospects" (1951), Milton Friedman also uses the term to describe the post-WWII model of state-managed capitalist economy. Michel Foucault discusses post-WWII capitalism as "neoliberalism" in his 1978–1979 lectures at the Collège de France, also in fact criticizing welfare capitalism.

8. Thatcher borrowed the phrase "there is no alternative" from Herbert Spencer's formulation of Social Darwinism a century earlier.

5. PRECARITY CAPITALISM

1. I have referred to this modality as "reorganized capitalism" (Azmanova 2010) and "aggregative capitalism" (Azmanova 2013a) to set it apart from the previous, neoliberal form that Offe, Lash, and Urry named "disorganized capitalism" or to highlight the rather peculiar function public authority performs in aggregating opportunities to actors who already

have competitive advantage in the global economy while allocating risks to society. I have here adopted the label "precarity capitalism" to bring into focus the massification of insecurity as its distinctive feature. The dynamic nature of capitalism, captured well in Schumpeter's notion "creative destruction," entails ongoing destabilization. However, for the first time economic and social uncertainty have become a distinctive feature of the social order.

2. The Lisbon Strategy was a ten-year action plan for economic development adopted by EU member states' leaders in March 2000. It pledged to make the EU, by 2010, "the most competitive and dynamic knowledge-based economy in the world" (EC 2000).

3. In the United States, the surge in high-tech capital investment began in 1993. See Federal Reserve Chairman Alan Greenspan's testimony before the Committee on Banking and Financial Services, U.S. House of Representatives, July 22, 1999, https://www.federalreserve.gov /boarddocs/hh/1999/July/testimony.htm.

4. The megadeals are led by the U.S. media and telecoms sector. Worldwide deal volumes in early 2018 were at their highest since Thomson Reuters began keeping data on mergers and acquisitions in 1980. James Fontanella-Khan and Arash Massoudi, "Global Dealmaking Reaches $2.5tn as US Megadeals Lift Volumes," *Financial Times*, June 28, 2018, https://www.ft.com/content/fc30ca5e-7a1d-11e8-8e67-1e1a0846c475.

5. Among sectors of the "old economy," the "resource" industries (extraction and trade of natural resources) have avoided this logic so far due to ever-increasing global demands for energy.

6. An example at hand is the "sweetheart" tax deal the Irish government has given to the technology giant Apple, which it has allowed to pay tax at a rate of 3.8 percent on $200 billion of overseas profits over ten years. In September 2016, the European Commission ruled that was a violation of the EU prohibition of state aid and ordered the company to pay billions of euros in taxes to the Irish state. Significantly, the Irish government, with broad support by both incumbent and oppositional political forces, launched an appeal against the ruling.

7. See "European Defence Fund and EU Defence Industrial Development Programme," https://ec.europa.eu/info/law/better-regulation /initiatives/com-2017–294_en.

8. Credit default swaps (CDS) have existed since the early 1990s, but their use increased rapidly between 2003 and 2007 (Kim 2013).

9. Karl Polanyi (1944) notes the fictitious nature of the commodification of land, labor, and money—that is, that these are entities that by their very essence are not properly susceptible to commodification (production exclusively for market exchange). I believe Jean-François Lyotard (1984, 4) was the first to address the emerging commodification of knowledge (being produced in order to be sold) in advanced capitalist societies, thus adding a fourth fictitious commodity.

10. Neither was it brought on by profligacy, as is widely believed. Spain and Ireland stood out for their low ratios of debt to Gross Domestic Product before the 2008 crisis, with ratios well below Germany's.

11. William James, "May Says Ready to Curb Human Rights Laws to Fight Extremism," Reuters, June 6, 2017.

12. For a detailed discussion of this condition of being stuck and its institutional and socio-psychological intricacies, see Hage 2009.

13. The Single Act (a revision of the 1957 Treaty of Rome with which the European Communities were established) set the objective of establishing a single market among member states by December 31, 1992.

14. Open markets are about trade policy. Free market (laissez-faire) is about the state of domestic production and exchange. Thus, one can imagine a configuration that combines an integrated market among EU member states through lifting interstate trade barriers, yet maintaining strong public sector and protected labor markets domestically. This would create a trans-European social market economy, which is currently not the case.

15. The principle of supremacy, or primacy of EU law, stipulates that the laws of the EU member states that conflict with the laws of the European Union should be considered void so that the latter can take effect. The doctrine that EU law is an independent source that cannot be overridden by domestic legal provisions without being deprived of its character as community law emerged in a series of European Court of Justice decisions, starting with Costa v. ENEL in 1964.

16. In the two cases, the European Court of Justice ruled that trade unions' rights to take collective action or to make foreign service providers respect certain minimum working conditions are limited by the EU's

principles of freedom of movement and establishment. The court effectively placed market freedom over social rights. *Official Journal of the European Union*, February 23, 2008, 10.

17. This is to replace the existing European Financial Stabilization Mechanism and the European Financial Stability Facility, vehicles for financial assistance to EU member states in financial difficulties, on condition that they adopt macroeconomic adjustment programs centered on product- and labor-market liberalization agreed by the European Commission and the European Central Bank (ECB).

18. The Fiscal Compact demands member states to enact laws requiring national budgets to be in balance or in surplus, effectively imposing austerity politics, at least in the short-term. These provisions were introduced in the Treaty on Stability, Coordination and Governance in the Economic and Monetary Union, signed on March 2, 2012 by all member states of the European Union except the United Kingdom and the Czech Republic.

19. A perfect illustration of this phenomenon is Facebook's and Twitter's banning, under political and public pressure, far-right American conspiracy theorist Alex Jones and fake news website Infowars from their platforms. Notwithstanding the immediate benefits of cleansing the public space of toxic content, with this act Facebook and Twitter assumed the right to make a judgment on who has access to that public space—that is, to sanction its use. This is only empowering private economic actors at the expense of public authority, while creating the illusion that the former can effectively ensure that the information they allow to appear in the public space is truthful. This is an impossible task for such a vast space of communication.

20. I owe the analogy between *raison d'état* and *raison d'économie* to my student Cécile Maitre-Ferri.

21. The Research Frameworks of the EU also fund basic science ("blue skies research" with no immediately practical application and market benefits). My stress in this account is on the uneven distribution of investment risks and benefits between society and private economic actors fostered by the predominant approach to EU funding.

22. Andrew Feenberg (2017) traces the input of nonspecialized publics into the development and implementation of technology to argue that

scientific rationality is not impermeable to the empirically grounded judgments of democratic publics. This allows him to close the gap between scientific rationality and everyday experience that had presented technology (and technocratic rule) as impervious to democracy. The process, often initiated in street protests, passes through hearings and lawsuits to culminate in new regulations that affect both the development and application of technology.

23. John F. Kennedy, during his service as senator, opposed the 1957 Civil Rights Act, aligning with the Democratic Party's segregationist Southern committee chairmen. Only the civil rights movement's "sustained, disciplined, sometimes brutality-provoking marches persuaded Kennedy to recast the public narrative about race and American identity" (Sleeper 2017).

24. Jodi Dean (2009) has argued that networked communications technologies are profoundly depoliticizing in the current political-economic formation, which she names "communicative capitalism."

6. WHAT IS AILING THE 99 PERCENT?

1. The fact that recruitment of *drivers* is racism-free is perfectly compatible with the fact that, like most Silicon Valley companies, Uber has few women and individuals from ethnic minorities in leadership positions.

2. Note that the academic journal *Loisir et Société/Society and Leisure* (Presses de l'Université du Québec) was established in 1978, reflecting a growing scientific interest in leisure time as a socially significant phenomenon.

3. Among the plethora of excellent works on this, I would single out Castells (1996), Boltanski and Chiapello (1999), and Haskel and Westlake (2017) as articulating most clearly the novel features of the so-called "new economy" of open borders and intense technological innovation.

4. I have discussed this first contradiction of contemporary capitalism and its social implications in Azmanova (2012c) and am reproducing some of the argument and supporting evidence here.

5. Judith Butler (2004) has drawn the distinction between *precariousness* as a general human condition of vulnerability, rooted in our interdependence on each other, and *precarity*, which is socially generated

vulnerability resulting from social marginalization, poverty, economic insecurity, political disenfranchisement, and/or violence. A distinctive feature of precarity, in this account, is its unequal distribution: it afflicts only some groups. Holmes (2010), Marazzi (2010), and Fumagalli and Mezzadra (2010) address precarization as an element in the transformation of capitalism. Paul Apostolidis (2017, 3) has argued that the features of precarious lives he records in his study of Latino day laborers are spreading well above the bottom class strata: "If precarity names the special plight of the world's most virulently oppressed human beings, it also denotes a near-universal complex of unfreedom." For a comprehensive discussion of the phenomenon and the usages of the term, see della Porta et al. (2015).

6. Work-related anxiety has increased in law firms as a result of the persistent long-term downturn in demand for their services and the use of technology over time to replace human resources in law firms. Thomas S. Clay and Eric A. Seeger, "Law Firms in Transition 2017: An Altman Weil Flash Survey," http://www.altmanweil.com/LFiT 2017/.

7. Economic suicides triggered by job loss, debt, and foreclosure during the Great Recession in Europe and North America have increased (Reeves, McKee, and Stuckler 2014). However, workplace suicides are a separate category. They are triggered by long working hours, hostile working conditions, competition, and employment uncertainty and are typically committed at work. According to the U.S. Bureau of Labor Statistics, workplace suicides have increased in recent years, even as the overall number of workplace fatalities have steadily declined (Harris 2016).

8. To the question "What would you do differently if you had five more years to live?," 64 percent responded that they would travel more, 61 percent would spend more time with their families, and only 3 percent would work harder to provide for their families. Two-thirds of those interviewed said that achieving financial security was the whole point of working to build wealth. Only the very wealthy (those with five million dollars or more) felt they had enough to be secure.

9. The sixteen countries are: Algeria, Canada, Costa Rica, Ethiopia, FYR Macedonia, Guatemala, Indonesia, Japan, Malaysia, Montenegro, Norway, Papua New Guinea, Peru, Samoa, Singapore, and Tonga.

7. GETTING UNSTUCK: OVERCOMING
CAPITALISM WITHOUT CRISIS,
REVOLUTION, OR UTOPIA

1. Survey by the Institute of Politics (IOP) at Harvard University, Spring 2016: http://iop.harvard.edu/youth-poll/harvard-iop-spring-2016-poll. In another poll by the European Broadcasting Union, more than half of respondents aged eighteen to thirty-four in the thirty-three European countries surveyed said "Yes" to the question "Would you actively participate in large scale uprising against the generation in power if it happened in the next days or months?" "Generation What?," EBU, Geneva, 2017, http://www.generation-what.eu/en/.

2. See my discussion of the relation between inequality and social privilege drawing on Alexis de Tocqueville in chapter 4.

3. For a rich socio-anthropological investigation of the effect of welfare reform on the way single parents, disabled people, and young job-seekers on welfare benefits relate to issues of citizenship, see Patrick 2017.

4. The proposed federal bill requires that employees in corporations with over $1 billion in tax receipts elect 40 percent of their board of directors, and that 75 percent of shareholders and directors must approve any political spending.

5. The National Railroad Passenger Corporation and Subsidiaries (Amtrak) is a U.S. government–owned corporation established in 1871. It is subjected to independent financial audit and is eligible for federal government funding. However, the price of the service is based on economic considerations of efficiency, not ones of "public service."

6. See, for instance, Unger 2006 and Reich 2010 and 2018.

7. See note 17 to chapter 3.

8. The events of May 1968 did not have the unqualified support of leftist intellectuals. In France, Louis Althusser (as well as the members of the Tel Quel group) reprimanded the student movement for not toeing the Communist Party line. In Germany, Adorno and Habermas cautioned that the student movement risked degenerating into "left fascism." Marcuse, who at the time held a position in California, endorsed the student movement (and opposed labelling it as left fascism), even as he

judged that the upheaval did not amount to a revolutionary situation. See Adorno and Marcuse 1969.

9. The Europe 2020 Project Bond Initiative was launched in 2016 by the European Commission and the European Investment Bank in an effort to boost the European economy by stimulating capital market financing for large-scale infrastructure projects in transport, energy, and information and communication technology. By providing a secure line of credit, the European bodies are hoping to offer "a peace of mind to institutional investors," as the policy document states. European Investment Bank, "The Europe 2020 Project Bond Initiative: Innovative Infrastructure Financing," http://www.eib.org/products/blending/project-bonds/index.htm.

10. I first used the term in Azmanova 2011b in an analysis of the conditions for effective multiculturalism.

11. For the most recent and comprehensive accounts to date of the idea of universal and unconditional basic income, see Standing 2017 and Van Parijs and Vanderborght 2017.

12. It is in this sense that Wolfgang Streeck (2008) has criticized the discourse on flexicurity, appealing for a return to a discourse on rights.

13. I refer to the "robot tax"—the idea that robots be taxed at a rate similar to that of workers—which was popularized by Microsoft founder Bill Gates in 2018 and taken up by U.S. congresswoman Alexandria Ocasio-Cortez and presidential candidate Andrew Yang.

14. For alternative nonproductivist models of social justice, see, for instance, Fitzpatrick (2004), Goodin (2001), Reich (2015, 2018), and Stiglitz (2016), who spell out policy ideas for reinventing our notions of well-being in pursuit of the common good. Guy Standing (2010, 2016), has drawn attention to the fact that capitalism valorizes work only as labor or income-generating activity, cautioning the Left to avoid the trap of this productivist romanticizing. James Chamberlain radicalizes this position further, urging us to abandon the view that community is constructed by work, whether paid or not. The model I articulate in this book has a place for these ideas, especially to the extent that they strike at the competitive production of profit as capitalism's constitutive dynamic.

15. For a detailed exposition of this argument, see Offe 2016.

CONCLUSION: THE RADICAL PRAGMATISM
OF BIDDING CAPITALISM FAREWELL

1. Another popular witticism from my youth under the Communist Party's dictatorship in my native Bulgaria put it this way: The difference between communism and capitalism is that under capitalism man exploits man; under communism it is the other way around. This remark is often attributed to John Kenneth Galbraith, but its source is unknown. What is important is that its popularity among East European dissidents captured well our healthy misgivings about both systems.

BIBLIOGRAPHY

Adorno, Theodor W. (1966) 1973. *Negative Dialectics*. Trans. E. B. Ashton. New York: Continuum.

——. 1970–1986. *Gesammelte Schriften in zwanzig Bänden* [*Complete Works*]. Ed. Rolf Tiedemann, with Gretel Adorno, Susan Buck-Morss, and Klaus Schultz. Frankfurt am Main: Suhrkamp, 2003.

——. 1976. "On the Logic of the Social Sciences." In Adorno et al. 1976, 105–22.

Adorno, Theodor W., Hans Albert, Ralf Dahrendorf, Jürgen Habermas, Harald Pilot, and Karl R. Popper. 1976. *The Positivist Dispute in German Sociology*. Trans. Glyn Adley and David Frisby. London: Heinemann Educational Books.

Adorno, Theodor W., and Herbert Marcuse. 1969. "Correspondence on the German Student Movement." *New Left Review* 233, no. 1 (January–February 1999): 123–36.

Allen, Amy. 2015. "Emancipation Without Utopia: Subjection, Modernity, and the Normative Claims of Feminist Critical Theory." *Hypatia* 30, no. 3: 513–29.

Apostolidis, Paul. 2018. *Migrant Day Laborers and the Politics of Precarity*. Oxford: Oxford University Press.

Arato, Andrew. 1982. "Political Sociology and the Critique of Politics." In *The Essential Frankfurt School Reader*, ed. Andrew. Arato and Eike Gebhardt, 3–25. New York: Continuum.

Atkinson, Anthony. 2015. *Inequality: What Can Be Done?* Cambridge, MA: Harvard University Press.

Azmanova, Albena. 2004. "The Mobilization of the European Left in the Early 21st Century." *European Journal of Sociology* 45, no. 2: 273–306.

——. 2010. "Capitalism Reorganized: Social Justice After Neo-Liberalism." *Constellations: An International Journal of Critical and Democratic Theory* 17, no. 3: 390–406.

——. 2011a. "After the Left-Right (Dis)continuum: Globalization and the Remaking of Europe's Ideological Geography." *International Political Sociology* 5, no. 4: 384–407.

——. 2011b. "Against the Politics of Fear: On Deliberation, Inclusion, and the Political Economy of Trust." *Philosophy and Social Criticism* 37, no. 2: 401–12.

——. 2011c. "Social Harm, Political Judgment, and the Pragmatics of Universal Justification." In *Philosophical Dimensions of Human Rights: Some Contemporary Views*, ed. Claudio Corradetti, 107–23. Oxford: Springer.

——. 2012a. "De-Gendering Social Justice in the 21st Century: An Immanent Critique of Neoliberal Capitalism." *European Journal of Social Theory* 15, no. 2: 143–56.

——. 2012b. *The Scandal of Reason: A Critical Theory of Political Judgment*. New York: Columbia University Press.

——. 2012c. "Social Justice and Varieties of Capitalism: An Immanent Critique." *New Political Economy* 17, no. 4: 445–63.

——. 2013a. "The 'Crisis of Capitalism' and the State—More Powerful, Less Responsible, Invariably Legitimate." In *Semantics of Statebuilding: Language, Meanings, and Sovereignty*, ed. Nicolas Lemay-Hébert, Nicholas Onuf, Vojin Rakić, and Petar Bojanić, 150–62. London: Routledge.

——. 2013b. "The Crisis of Europe: Democratic Deficit and Eroding Sovereignty—Not Guilty." *Law and Critique* 24, no. 1: 23–38.

——. 2014. "Crisis? Capitalism Is Doing Very Well. How Is Critical Theory?" *Constellations* 21, no. 3: 351–65.

——. 2016a. "Empowerment as Surrender: How Women Lost the Battle for Emancipation as They Won Equality and Inclusion." *Social Research* 83, no. 3 (Fall): 749–76.

——. 2016b. "The Right to Politics and Republican Non-Domination." *Philosophy and Social Criticism* 42 (May–June): 465–75.

——. 2018a. "The Populist Catharsis: On the Revival of the Political." *Philosophy and Social Criticism* 44, no. 4: 399–411.

———. 2018b. "Relational, Structural, and Systemic Forms of Power: The 'Right to Justification' Confronting Three Types of Domination." *Journal of Political Power* 11, no. 1 (February): 68–78.

Baldwin, Richard. 2019. *The Globotics Upheaval: Globalization, Robotics, and the Future of Work*. London: Orion.

Barboza, David. 2017. "How a Silicon Valley Firm Is Aiding China's Ambitions." *New York Times*, August 6, 2017, Sunday Business.

Bauman, Zygmunt. 2016. *Strangers at Our Door*. Malden, MA: Polity.

Beck, Ulrich. 1992. *Risk Society: Towards a New Modernity*. London: Sage.

Beck, Ulrich, and Elisabeth Beck-Gernsheim. 2002. *Individualization: Institutionalized Individualism and Its Social and Political Consequences*. London: Sage.

Bell, David N. F., and David G. Blanchflower. 2018. "Underemployment in the U.S. and Europe." NBER Working Paper No. 24927. https://www.nber.org/papers/w24927

Benhabib, Seyla. 1986. *Critique, Norm, and Utopia: A Study of the Foundations of Critical Theory*. New York: Columbia University Press.

Blanchard, Kathryn D. 2010. *The Protestant Ethic, or the Spirit of Capitalism: Christians, Freedom, and Free Markets*. Eugene, OR: Cascade Books.

Bloch, Ernst. 1988. *The Utopian Function of Art and Literature*. Cambridge, MA: MIT Press.

Bobbio, Norberto. 1996. *Left and Right: The Significance of a Political Distinction*. Trans. Allan Cameron. Chicago: University of Chicago Press.

Boltanski, Luc, and Eve Chiapello. 1999. *The New Spirit of Capitalism*. London: Verso, 2005.

Bourdieu, Pierre. 1986. "The Forms of Capital." In *Handbook of Theory and Research for the Sociology of Education*, ed. John G. Richardson, 241–58. New York: Greenwood.

Brown, Wendy. 1995. *States of Injury: Power and Freedom in Late Modernity*. Princeton, NJ: Princeton University Press.

———. 2015. *Undoing the Demos: Neoliberalism's Stealth Revolution*. New York: Zone Books.

Butler, Judith. 2004. *Precarious Life: The Powers of Mourning and Violence*. New York: Verso.

Cabrita, Jorge, Simon Boehmer, and Camilla Galli da Bino. 2016. "Working Time Developments in the 21st Century: Work Duration and Its

Regulation in the EU." Eurofound: European Foundation for the Improvement of Living and Working Conditions, report EF1573. https:// www.eurofound.europa.eu/publications/report/2016/industrial-rela tions-law-and-regulation/working-time-developments-in-the-21st -century-work-duration-and-its-regulation-in-the-eu.

Castells, Manuel. 1996. *The Rise of the Network Society*. Oxford: Wiley-Blackwell.

Chamberlain, James A. 2018. *Undoing Work, Rethinking Community: A Critique of the Social Function of Work*. Ithaca, NY: Cornell University Press.

Clark, Terry N., and Vincent Hoffmann-Martinot, eds. 1998. *The New Political Culture*. Boulder, CO: Westview Press.

Consortium of Research Institutes in Climate Change (CRICC). 2018. "Aligning National and International Climate Targets." Report of Grantham Research Institute on Climate Change and the ESRC Centre for Climate Change Economics and Policy. London: London School of Economics. October 29, 2018. http://www.lse.ac.uk/GranthamInstitute /publication/targets/.

Corfe, Robert. 2010. *The Future of Politics with the Demise of the Left/Right Confrontational System*. Suffolk, UK: Arena Books.

Cox, Robert. 1981. "Social Forces, States, and World Orders: Beyond International Relations Theory." *Millennium: Journal of International Studies* 10, no. 2: 126–55.

Crouch, Colin. 2011. *The Strange Non-Death of Neo-Liberalism*. Cambridge: Polity.

——. 2017. *Can Neoliberalism Be Saved from Itself?* London: Social Europe Editions.

Dean, Jodi. 2009. *Democracy and Other Neoliberal Fantasies: Communicative Capitalism and Left Politics*. Durham, NC: Duke University Press.

Della Porta, Donatella, Sakari Hänninen, Martti Siisiäinen, and Tiina Silvasti. 2015. "The Precarization Effect." In *The New Social Division: Making and Unmaking Precariousness*, ed. Donatella della Porta, Sakari Hänninen, Martti Siisiäinen, and Tiina Silvasti. London: Palgrave Macmillan.

Derrida, Jacques. 1983. "Economies of the Crisis." In *Negotiations: Interventions and Interviews, 1971–2001*, ed. and trans. Elizabeth Rottenberg, 69–73. Stanford, CA: Stanford University Press, 2002.

Desmond, Matthew. 2016. *Evicted: Poverty and Profit in the American City*. New York: Crown.

Deutscher, Penelope, and Christina Lafont, eds. 2017. *Critical Theory in Critical Times: Transforming the Political and Economic Order.* New York: Columbia University Press.

Dinmore, Guy. 2008. "Man in the News: Umberto Bossi." *Financial Times,* April 18, 2008.

Dorling, Danny. 2015. *Inequality and the 1%.* London: Verso.

Engels, Friedrich. 1845. *The Conditions of the Working-Class in England in 1844.* Trans. F. K. Wischnewetzky. New York: Cosimo, 2008.

Esping-Andersen, Gøsta. 1990. *The Three Worlds of Welfare Capitalism.* Cambridge: Polity Press.

European Commission (EC). 2005a. "The European Constitution: Post-Referendum Survey in France." *Flash Eurobarometer* 171 (June).

——. 2005b. "The European Constitution: Post-Referendum Survey in the Netherlands." *Flash Eurobarometer* 172 (June).

——. 2011. "Horizon 2020." European Commission. Brussels: https://ec .europa.eu/programmes/horizon2020/.

European Parliament (EP). 2017. "EU Migrant Crisis: Facts and Figures." June 30, 2017. http://www.europarl.europa.eu/news/en/headlines/society /20170629STO78630/eu-migrant-crisis-facts-and-figures.

European Risk Observatory. 2008. "Work-Related Stress: New Challenges in a Changing Workplace." Report of the European Agency for Safety and Health at Work (OSHA). European Risk Observatory, Brussels, January 31, 2008.

European Trade Union Institute. 2018. "One in Every Five European Workers Endures Work-Related Stress." May 3, 2018. https://www.etui.org /Topics/Health-Safety-working-conditions/News-list/One-in-every -five-European-workers-endures-work-related-stress.

Feenberg, Andrew. 2017. *Technosystem: The Social Life of Reason.* Cambridge, MA: Harvard University Press.

Finlayson, Gordon. 2014. "Hegel, Adorno, and Immanent Criticism." *British Journal for the History of Philosophy* 22, no. 6: 1142–66.

Fitzpatrick, Tony. 2004. "A Post-Productivist Future for Social Democracy?" *Social Policy and Society* 3, no. 3: 213–22.

Fleming, Peter. 2017. *The Death of Homo Economicus: Work, Debt, and the Myth of Endless Accumulation.* London: Pluto Press.

Forst, Rainer. 2011. *The Right to Justification: Elements of a Constructivist Theory of Justice.* Trans. Jeffrey Flynn. New York: Columbia University Press.

Frankfurt, Harry G. 2015. *On Inequality*. Princeton, NJ: Princeton University Press.

Franzini, Maurizio, Elena Granaglia, and Michele Raitano. 2016. *Extreme Inequalities in Contemporary Capitalism: Should We Be Concerned About the Rich?* Cham, Switzerland: Springer.

Fraser, Nancy. 2003. "On the Place of Experience in Critical Theory." *Dissent* (January).

——. 2009. "Feminism, Capitalism, and the Cunning of History." *New Left Review* 56.

——. 2013. "A Triple Movement: Parsing the Politics of Crisis After Polanyi." *New Left Review* 81: 119–32.

——. 2014a. "Behind Marx's Hidden Abode: For an Expanded Conception of Capitalism." *New Left Review* 86: 55–72.

——. 2014b. "Can Society Be Commodities All the Way Down? Post-Polanyian Reflections on Capitalist Crisis." *Economy and Society* 43, no. 4: 541–58.

——. 2015. "Legitimation Crisis? On the Political Contradictions of Financialized Capitalism." *Critical Historical Studies* 2, no. 2: 157–89.

——. 2017a. "Against Progressive Neoliberalism, a New Progressive Populism." *Dissent*, January 28.

——. 2017b. "The End of Progressive Neoliberalism." *Dissent*, January 2.

Fraser, Nancy, and Rahel Jaeggi. 2018. *Capitalism: A Conversation in Critical Theory*. Cambridge: Polity.

Friedman, Benjamin M. 2005. *The Moral Consequences of Economic Growth*. New York: Knopf.

Fuchs, Dieter, and Hans-Dieter Klingemann. 1990. "The Left-Right Schema." In *Continuities in Political Action: A Longitudinal Study of Political Orientations in Three Western Democracies*, ed. M. Kent Jennings and Jan W. van Deth, 203–34. Berlin: De Gruyter.

Fumagalli, Andrea, and Sandro Mezzadra, eds. 2010. *Crisis in the Global Economy: Financial Markets, Social Struggles and New Political Scenarios*. Los Angeles: Semiotext(e).

Geishecker, Ingo, and Holger Görg. 2007. *Winners and Losers: A Micro-Level Analysis of International Outsourcing and Wages*. Discussion Paper 6484. London: Center for Economic Policy Research.

Geuss, Raymond. 1981. *The Idea of Critical Theory: Habermas and the Frankfurt School*. Cambridge: Cambridge University Press.

Giddens, Anthony. 1994. *Beyond Left and Right: The Future of Radical Politics*. Stanford, CA: Stanford University Press.

Gilens, Martin. 2014. *Affluence and Influence: Economic Inequality and Political Power in America*. Princeton, NJ: Princeton University Press.

Gilens, Martin, and Benjamin I. Page. 2014. "Testing Theories of American Politics: Elites, Interest Groups, and Average Citizens." *Perspectives on Politics* 12, no. 3 (September): 564–81.

Goodin, Robert E. 2001. "Work and Welfare: Towards a Post-Productivist Welfare Regime." *British Journal of Political Science* 31, no. 1: 13–39.

Goodin, Robert E., James M. Rice, Antti Parpo, and Line Eriksson. 2008. *Discretionary Time: A New Measure of Freedom*. Cambridge: Cambridge University Press.

Gramsci, Antonio. 1929–1935. *Prison Notebooks*. 3 vols. Trans. Joseph A. Buttigieg. New York: Columbia University Press, 2011.

Gray, John. 1998. *False Dawn: The Delusions of Global Capitalism*. London: Granta.

Greenberg, Edward S. 1974. *Serving the Few: Corporate Capitalism and the Bias of Government Policy*. New York: Wiley.

Grundy, George W., and Dylan Avery. 2017. *Death of a Nation: 9/11 and the Rise of Fascism in America*. New York: Skyhorse.

Habermas, Jürgen. 1973. *Legitimation Crisis*. Trans. Thomas McCarthy. Boston: Beacon Press.

——. 1981. *Lifeworld and System: A Critique of Functionalist Reason*. Vol. 2 of *A Theory of Communicative Action*. Boston: Beacon Press.

Hage, Ghassan. 2009. "Waiting Out the Crisis: On Stuckedness and Governmentality." In *Waiting*, ed. Ghassan Hage, 97–106. Victoria: Melbourne University Press.

Hall, Peter, and David Soskise, eds. 2001. *Varieties of Capitalism: The Institutional Foundations of Comparative Advantage*. Oxford: Oxford University Press.

Hardt, Michael, and Antonio Negri. 2004. *Multitude: War and Democracy in the Age of Empire*. New York: Penguin.

——. 2017. *Assembly*. Oxford: Oxford University Press.

Harman, Chris. 2007. "Theorising Neoliberalism." *International Socialism* 117 (December 18). http://isj.org.uk/theorising-neoliberalism/.

Harris, Reginald. 2016. "Suicide in the Workplace." *Monthly Labor Review*. U.S. Bureau of Labor Statistics, December 2016. https://stats.bls.gov/opub/mlr/2016/article/pdf/suicide-in-the-workplace.pdf.

Hartmann, Martin, and Axel Honneth. 2006. "Paradoxes of Capitalism." *Constellations* 13, no. 1: 41–58.

Harvey, David. 2003. *The New Imperialism*. Oxford: Oxford University Press.

——. 2005. *A Brief History of Neoliberalism*. Oxford: Oxford University Press.

——. 2010. *The Enigma of Capital and the Crises of Capitalism*. Oxford: Oxford University Press.

——. 2014. *Seventeen Contradictions and the End of Capitalism*. London: Profile.

Haskel, Jonathan, and Stian Westlake. 2017. *Capitalism Without Capital: The Rise of the Intangible Economy*. Princeton, NJ: Princeton University Press.

Havel, Václav. (1984) 1991. "Politics and Conscience." In *Open Letters: Selected Prose, 1965–1990*, ed. Paul Wilson, 249–71. London: Faber and Faber.

——. (1986) 1991. "The Politics of Hope." In *Disturbing the Peace: A Conversation with Karel Hvizdala*, trans. Paul Wilson. London: Vintage.

Hayden, Tom. 1962. *The Port Huron Statement: The Visionary Call of the 1960s Revolution*. New York: Thunder's Mouth Press, 2005.

Held, David. 1999. *Global Transformations: Politics, Economics and Culture*. Stanford, CA: Stanford University Press.

——. 2016. *Global Politics After 9/11: Failed Wars, Fragmentation, and Authoritarianism*. London: Global Policy.

Held, David, and Anthony McGrew, eds. 2007. *Globalization Theory: Approaches and Controversies*. Cambridge: Polity.

Hellwig, Timothy, and David Samuels. 2007. "Voting in Open Economies: The Electoral Consequences of Globalisation." *Comparative Political Studies* 40, no. 3: 283–306.

——. 2017. *Assembly*. Oxford: Oxford University Press.

Hobsbawm, Eric. 1975. *The Age of Capital, 1848–1875*. London: Abacus.

Holmes, Brian. 2010. "Is It Written in the Stars? Global Finance, Precarious Destinies." *Ephemera: Theory & Politics in Organization* 10: 222–33.

Honneth, Axel. 2014. *Freedom's Right. The Social Foundations of Democratic Life*. Trans. Joseph Ganahl. New York: Columbia University Press.

Horkheimer, Max. 1937. "Traditional and Critical Theory." In *Critical Theory: Selected Essays*, trans. M. J. O'Connell, 188–243. New York: Continuum, 2002.

Inglehart, Ronald. 1977. *The Silent Revolution: Changing Values and Political Styles Among Western Publics*. Princeton, NJ: Princeton University Press.

——. 2008. "Changing Values Among Western Publics from 1970 to 2006." *West European Politics* 31: 130–46.

International Labour Organization (ILO). 2018a. "Unemployment and Decent Work Deficits to Remain High in 2018." January 22, 2018. http://www.ilo.org/global/about-the-ilo/newsroom/news/WCMS_615590.

——. 2018b. *The World Employment and Social Outlook: Trends 2018*. Geneva: ILO.

Jaeggi, Rahel. 2017. "A Wide Concept of the Economy: Economy as a Social Practice and the Critique of Capitalism." In *Critical Theory in Critical Times: Transforming the Political and Economic Order*, ed. Penelope Deutscher and Cristina Lafont, 160–80. New York: Columbia University Press.

Jay, Martin. 1984. *Adorno*. Cambridge, MA: Harvard University Press.

Judis, John. 2016. *The Populist Explosion: How the Great Recession Transformed American and European Politics*. New York: Columbia Global Reports.

Kant, Emmanuel. (1795) 1991. "Perpetual Peace: A Philosophical Sketch." In *Political Writings*, ed. H. S. Reiss, 93–124. Cambridge: Cambridge University Press.

Kapstein, Ethan B. 2000. "Winners and Losers in the Global Economy." *International Organization* 54, no. 2: 359–84.

Keane, John. 2009. *The Life and Death of Democracy*. London: Simon & Schuster.

Keynes, John Maynard. (1930) 1963. "Economic Possibilities for Our Grandchildren." In *Essays in Persuasion*. New York: Norton.

Kim, Gi H. 2013. "Credit Default Swaps, Strategic Default, and the Cost of Corporate Debt." Warwick Business School Finance Group Working Papers, no. 13–12. http://web.warwick.ac.uk/fac/soc/financeRepec/Repec/2013/Kim2013CDSSDCCD.pdf

Kitschelt, Herbert. 2004. *Diversification and Reconfiguration of Party Systems in Postindustrial Democracies*. Bonn, Germany: Friedrich Ebert Stiftung.

Klein, Steven. 2019 (forthcoming). *The Work of Politics: Making a Democratic Welfare State*. Cambridge: Cambridge University Press.

Kriesi, Hanspeter, Edgar Grande, Romain Lachat, Martin Dolezal, Simon Bornschier, and Tim Frey. 2006. "Globalization and the Transformation of the National Political Space: Six European Countries Compared." *European Journal of Political Research* 45: 921–56.

Kuhn, Peter, and Fernando Lozano. 2005. "The Expanding Workweek? Understanding Trends in Long Work Hours Among U.S. Men, 1979–2004." NBER Working Paper No. 11895. https://www.nber.org/papers/w11895.pdf

Laclau, Ernesto, and Chantal Mouffe. 1985. *Hegemony and Socialist Strategy.* London: Verso.

Lagarde, Christine. 2015. "Economic Inclusion and Financial Integrity—An Address to the Conference on Inclusive Capitalism." International Monetary Fund, May 27, 2014. https://www.imf.org/en/News/Articles/2015/09/28/04/53/sp052714.

——. 2017. "IMF's Christine Lagarde: 'Inequality Is Rising.'" BBC interview with Christine Lagarde. http://www.bbc.com/news/av/business-27595151/imf-s-christine-lagarde-inequality-is-rising.

Laponce, Jean. 1981. *Left and Right: The Topography of Political Perceptions.* Toronto: University of Toronto Press.

Lash, Scott, and John Urry. 1987. *The End of Organized Capitalism.* Madison: University of Wisconsin Press.

Lee, Sangheon, Deirdre McCann, and Jon C. Messenger. 2007. *Working Time Around the World: Trends in Working Hours, Laws, and Policies in a Global Comparative Perspective.* Geneva: International Labour Organisation.

Leibfried, Stephan. 2010. "Social Policy. Left to the Judges and the Markets?" In *Policy Making in the European Union*, ed. H. Wallace, W. Wallace, and M. A. Pollack, 243–78. Oxford: Oxford University Press.

Lilla, Mark. 2016. "The End of Identity Politics." *New York Times*, November 18, 2016.

——. 2017. *The Once and Future Liberal: After Identity Politics.* New York: Harper.

Lipset, Seymour M., and Stein Rokkan. 1967. "Cleavage Structures, Party Systems and Voter Alignments: An Introduction." In *Party Systems and Voter Alignments: Cross-National Perspectives*, ed. S. M. Lipset and S. Rokkan. New York: Free Press.

Lyotard, Jean François. 1984. *The Postmodern Condition: A Report on Knowledge*, Minneapolis: University of Minnesota Press.

Mair, Peter. 2007a. "The Challenge to Party Government." EUI Working Papers, SPS No. 2007/09. Florence: European University Institute.

——. 2007b. "Left–Right Orientations." In *The Oxford Handbook of Political Behaviour*, ed. Russell J. Dalton and Hans-Dieter Klingemann, 206–22. Oxford: Oxford University Press.

Majone, Giandomenico. 1990. *Deregulation or Re-Regulation? Regulatory Reform in Europe and the United States.* London: Francis Pinter.

Mann, Michael. 1986–2012. *The Sources of Social Power*. 3 vols. Cambridge: Cambridge University Press.

Marazzi, Christian. 2010. *The Violence of Financial Capitalism*. Los Angeles: Semiotext(e)

Marcuse, Herbert. (1932) 1973. "The Foundation of Historical Materialism." In *Studies in Critical Philosophy*. Boston: Beacon Press.

——. (1933) 1973. "On the Philosophical Foundations of the Concept of Labor in Economics." *Telos* 16: 9–37.

——. 1964. *One-Dimensional Man: Studies in the Ideology of Advanced Industrial Society*. Boston: Beacon Press.

Marx, Karl. (1845) 1969. *Theses on Feuerbach*. In *Marx/Engels, Selected Works*, vol. 1., trans. W. Lough, 13–15. Moscow: Progress Publishers.

——. 1848. "Manifesto of the Communist Party." In *Marx/Engels, Selected Works*, vol. 1.

——. (1857) 1973. *Grundrisse: Foundations of the Critique of Political Economy*. Trans. Martin Nicolaus. London: Pelican Marx Library.

——. (1859a) 1970. *A Contribution to the Critique of Political Economy*. Trans. S. W. Ryazanskaya. Moscow: Progress Publishers.

——. 1859b. "Population, Crime, and Pauperism." *New York Daily Tribune*, September 16, 1859.

——. (1867) 1965. *Capital*. Vol. 1: *The Process of Production of Capital*. Trans. Samuel Moore and Edward Aveling. Moscow: Progress Publishers.

——. (1885) 1956. *Capital*. Vol. 2: *The Process of Circulation of Capital*. Ed. Frederick Engels. Trans. I. Lasker. Moscow: Progress Publishers.

——. (1894) 1981. *Capital*. Vol. 3: *The Process of Capitalist Production as a Whole*. Ed. Frederick Engels. Trans. D. Fernbach. London: Penguin and New Left Review.

Marx, Karl, and Friedrich Engels. 1962. *Selected Works*. 2 vols. Moscow: Foreign Language Publishing House.

Mascherini, Massimiliano. 2017. "Long-Term Unemployed Youth: Characteristics and Policy Responses." Eurofound: European Foundation for the Improvement of Living and Working Conditions, December 14, 2017. https://www.eurofound.europa.eu/publications/blog/long-term-unemployed-youth-the-legacy-of-the-crisis.

Mason, Paul. 2015. *PostCapitalism: A Guide to Our Future*. London: Penguin.

Mattick, Paul. 2011. *Business as Usual: The Economic Crisis and the Failure of Capitalism*. London: Reaktion Books.

Mazzucato, Mariana. 2013. *The Entrepreneurial State: Debunking Public vs. Private Sector Myths*. London: Anthem Press.

McGinnity, Frances, and Emma Calvert. 2009. "Work-Life Conflict and Social Inequality in Western Europe." *Social Indicators Research* 93, no. 3: 489–508.

McKnight, David. 2005. *Beyond Right and Left: New Politics and the Culture Wars*. Crow's Nest, NSW, Australia: Allen & Unwin.

Mouffe, Chantal. 2005. *On the Political*. London: Routledge.

——. 2018. *For a Left Populism*. London: Verso.

Norris, Pippa. 2005. *Radical Right: Voters and Parties in the Electoral Market*. Cambridge: Cambridge University Press.

Obama, Barack. 2006. Keynote address at the launch of the Brookings Institute's Hamilton Project, April 5, 2006. Viewable at YouTube, "Barack Obama at the Launch of the Brookings Institute's Hamilton Project," posted by heckofjob, November 30, 2009, https://youtu.be/P-5Y74FrDCc.

Offe, Claus. 1985. *Disorganized Capitalism: Contemporary Transformations of Work and Politics*. Cambridge: Polity.

——. 2016. *Europe Entrapped*. Cambridge: Polity Press.

Oppenhuis, Erik. 1995. *Voting Behavior in Europe: A Comparative Analysis of Electoral Participation and Party Choice*. Amsterdam: Het Spinhuis.

Palermo, Giulio. 2017. "Competition: A Marxist View." *Cambridge Journal of Economics* 41, no. 6: 1559–85.

Patrick, Ruth. 2017. *For Whose Benefit? The Everyday Realities of Welfare Reform*. Bristol, UK: Policy.

Perrineau, Pascal. 2002. "Les évolutions de la Ve République: L'affaiblissement de l'antagonisme gauche/droite." *Cahiers francais* 300, no. 1: 48–54.

Piketty, Thomas. 2014. *Capital in the Twenty-First Century*. Cambridge, MA: Harvard University Press.

Polanyi, Karl. 1944. *The Great Transformation: The Political and Economic Origins of Our Time*. Boston: Beacon Press, 1957.

Postone, Moishe. 1993. *Time, Labor, and Social Domination: A Reinterpretation of Marx's Critical Theory*. New York: Cambridge University Press.

Przeworski, Adam. 2012. "Economic Inequality, Political Inequality, and Redistribution." *Brazilian Political Science Review* 6, no. 1: 11–36.

Quart, Alissa. 2018. *Squeezed: Why Our Families Can't Afford America.* New York: HarperCollins.

Reed, Alec. 2011. *Capitalism Is Dead—Peoplism Rules: Creating Success Out of Corporate Chaos.* London: McGraw-Hill.

Reeves, Aaron, Martin McKee, and David Stuckler. 2014. "Economic Suicides in the Great Recession in Europe and North America." *British Journal of Psychiatry* 205, no. 3: 246–47.

Reich, Robert B. 2007. *Supercapitalism: The Transformation of Business, Democracy, and Everyday Life.* New York: Vintage.

——. 2010. *Aftershock: The Next Economy and America's Future.* New York: Alfred A. Knopf.

——. 2015. *Saving Capitalism: For the Many, Not the Few.* New York: Alfred A. Knopf.

——. 2018. *The Common Good.* New York: Alfred A. Knopf.

Reid-Henry, Simon. 2015. *The Political Origins of Inequality: Why a More Equal World Is Better for Us All.* Chicago: University of Chicago Press.

Rhodes, Martin. 2001. "The Political Economy of Social Pacts: Competitive Corporatism and European Welfare Reform." In *The New Politics of the Welfare State,* ed. Paul Pierson, 165–94. Oxford: Oxford University Press.

Roberts, Alasdair. 2013. *The End of Protest: How Free-Market Capitalism Learned to Control Dissent.* Ithaca, NY: Cornell University Press.

Roberts, Michael. 2016. *The Long Depression: Marxism and the Global Crisis of Capitalism.* Chicago: Haymarket Books.

Rorty, Richard. 1996. "What's Wrong with Rights?" *Harper's Magazine* (June): 15–18.

Roth, Felix, Felicitas Nowak-Lehmann D., and Thomas Otter. 2011. "Has the Financial Crisis Shattered Citizens' Trust in National and European Governmental Institutions?" CEPS Working Document No. 343, June 2011. https://www.ceps.eu/ceps-publications/has-financial-crisis -shattered-citizens-trust-national-and-european-governmental/.

Rueda, David. 2006. "Social Democracy and Active Labour-Market Policies: Insiders, Outsiders and the Politics of Employment Promotion." *British Journal of Political Science* 36, no. 3: 385–406.

Sarkar, Saral. 2014. *The Crises of Capitalism: A Different Study of Political Economy.* Trans. Graciela Calderon. Berkeley, CA: Counterpoint.

Sartori, Giovanni. 1976. *Parties and Party Systems: A Framework for Analysis.* Cambridge: Cambridge University Press.

Sassen, Saskia. 2014. *Expulsions: Brutality and Complexity in the Global Economy.* Cambridge, MA: Harvard University Press.

Schattschneider, Elmer E. 1948. *The Struggle for Party and Government.* College Park: University of Maryland.

Schumpeter, Joseph A. 1928. "The Instability of Capitalism." *Economic Journal,* 38. Reprinted in *Essays: On Entrepreneurs, Innovations, Business Cycles, and the Evolution of Capitalism,* ed. R. V. Clemence, 47–72. New Brunswick, NJ: Transaction Publishers, 1989.

——. 1943. *Capitalism, Socialism, and Democracy.* London: Routledge, 2003.

Shaikh, Anwar. 2016. *Capitalism: Competition, Conflict, Crises.* Oxford: Oxford University Press.

Shiller, Robert. 2013. "Nobel-Winning Economist Warns: Rising Inequality a Problem." Interview with the Associated Press, October 15, 2013. http://www.telegram.com/article/20131015/NEWS/310149727.

Shklar, Judith N. 1992. *The Faces of Injustice.* New Haven, CT: Yale University Press.

Skocpol, Theda, Vanessa Williamson, and John Coggin. 2011. "The Tea Party and the Remaking of Republican Conservatism." *Perspectives on Politics* 9, no. 1: 25–43.

Sleeper, Jim. 2017. "Eyes Off the Prize." *Democracy,* August 17, 2017. https://democracyjournal.org/arguments/eyes-off-the-prize/.

Srnicek, Nick, and Alex Williams. 2015. *Inventing the Future: Postcapitalism and a World Without Work.* London: Verso.

Standing, Guy. 2010. *Work After Globalization: Building Occupational Citizenship.* Cheltenham, UK: Edward Elgar.

——. 2011. *The Precariat: The New Dangerous Class.* London: Bloomsbury.

——. 2016. *The Corruption of Capitalism: Why Rentiers Thrive and Work Does Not Pay.* London: Biteback.

——. 2017. *Basic Income: A Guide for the Open-Minded.* New Haven, CT: Yale University Press.

Steinem, Gloria. 2015. *My Life on the Road.* New York: Random House.

Stiglitz, Joseph E. 2003. *Globalization and Its Discontents.* New York: Norton.

———. 2015. *The Great Divide: Unequal Societies and What We Can Do About Them*. New York: Norton.

Streeck, Wolfgang. 1984. "Neo-Corporatist Industrial Relations and the Economic Crisis in West Germany." In *Order and Conflict in Contemporary Capitalism*, ed. John H. Goldthorpe, 291–314. Oxford: Oxford University Press.

———. 2009. *Re-Forming Capitalism: Institutional Change in the German Political Economy*. Oxford: Oxford University Press.

———. 2010. "Taking Capitalism Seriously: Toward an Institutionalist Approach to Contemporary Political Economy." MPIfG Discussion Paper 10/15.

———. 2014. *Buying Time: The Delayed Crisis of Democratic Capitalism*. London: Verso. First published in German by Suhrkamp, 2013.

———. 2016. *How Will Capitalism End? Essays on a Failing System*. London: Verso.

Sull, Don. 2009. "Survival in an Age of Turbulence." *Financial Times*, April 16, 2009.

Tepper, Jonathan, and Denise Hearn. 2018. *The Myth of Capitalism: Monopolies and the Death of Competition*. Hoboken, NJ: Wiley & Sons.

Thomassen, Jacques A. 1994. "Empirical Research into Political Representation: Failing Democracy or Failing Models?" In *Elections at Home and Abroad: Essays in Honour of Warren Miller*, ed. M. K. Jennings and T. E. Mann, 237–65. Ann Arbor: University of Michigan Press.

Tocqueville, Alexis de. (1835) 1990. *Democracy in America*. 2 vols. New York: Vintage Books.

Tolentino, Jia. 2017. "Charlottesville and the Effort to Downplay Racism in America." *New Yorker*, August 13, 2017.

Tufekci, Zeynep. 2017. *Twitter and Tear Gas: The Power and Fragility of Networked Protest*. New Haven, CT: Yale University Press.

UBS. 2015. "When Is Enough . . Enough? Why the Wealthy Can't Get Off the Treadmill." UBS Investor Watch.

Ughetto, Pascal. 2008. "Workplace Suicides Highlight Issue of Rising Stress Levels at Work." European Observatory of Working Life publication. January 13, 2008. https://www.eurofound.europa.eu/observatories/eurwork /articles/workplace-suicides-highlight-issue-of-rising-stress-levels-at -work.

Unger, Roberto. 2006. *The Left Alternative*. London: Verso.

Valéry, Paul. 1941. *Tel Quel*. Paris: Gallimard.

Van Parijs, Philippe, and Yannick Vanderborght. 2017. *Basic Income: A Radical Proposal for a Free Society and a Sane Economy*. Cambridge, MA: Harvard University Press.

Weber, Max. (1904–1905) 1992. *The Protestant Ethic and the Spirit of Capitalism*. Trans. Talcott Parsons. London: Routledge, 1992.

——. (1920) 1947. *The Theory of Social and Economic Organization*. Trans. A. M. Henderson and Talcott Parsons. Glencoe, IL: The Free Press.

——. (1922) 1978. *Economy and Society*. 2 vols. Ed. Guenther Roth and Claus Wittich. Berkeley: University of California Press.

Wilde, Oscar. (1891) 1912. *The Soul of Man Under Socialism*. London: Arthur L. Humphreys.

World Meteorological Organisation (WMO). 2019. "WMO Statement on the State of the Global Climate in 2018." https://library.wmo.int/index .php?lvl=notice_display&id=20799#.XLBET-gzZEY.

Yonnet, Paul. 1999. *Travail, loisir, temps libre et lien social*. Paris: Gallimard.

Žižek, Slavoj. 2018. *Like a Thief in Broad Daylight: Power in the Era of Post-Humanity*. London: Penguin/Allen Lane.

INDEX

Page numbers in *italics* denote illustrations or tables.

NEW DIRECTIONS IN CRITICAL THEORY

AMY ALLEN, GENERAL EDITOR